Other Titles by Thom Nickels

The Cliffs of Aries (Aegina Press, 1988)

Two Novellas: Walking Water & After All This
(Banned Books, 1989)

The Boy on the Bicycle (Starbooks Press, 1992-93)

Manayunk (Arcadia Publishing, 2001-02-03-04)

Gay and Lesbian Philadelphia (Arcadia, 2002-03-04)

Tropic of Libra (Starbooks Press, 2002)

Philadelphia Architecture (Arcadia Publishing, 2005)

OUT IN HISTORY

COLLECTED ESSAYS
by
THOM NICKELS

A STARbooks Press Publication

FLF/STARbooks Press
P. O. Box 2737
Sarasota, FL 34236-2737
Printed in the United States.

Cover photography provided by the Library of Congress. Gertrude Stein: Prints & Photographs Division, Carl Van Vechten Collection. Oscar Wilde: photo by Napoleon Sarony. James Baldwin: photo by Max Petrus. Jean Genet: New York World-Telegram and the Sun Newspaper Photograph Collection, photo by Jerry Bauer

Cover design: John Nail. Mr. Nail may be reached at: _tojonail@bellsouth.net_.

Book format: Michael Huxley.

Library of Congress Control Number: 2005926895
ISBN: 1-891855-58-1

Many thanks to Michael Huxley for his editorial expertise, to Joel Kaylor for his insights on Walt Whitman, to Al Patrick, Felice Picano, and most especially to Rocco Romagnoli.

CONTENTS

OUT IN HISTORY

—For Rocky

FORWARD

L et's be honest, only a few books are truly essential: a good dictionary, a fat cookbook, a one- or two-volume encyclopedia, and *The Joy of Gay Sex*. Today, we'd probably be wise to add a good legal guide, a car manual, and childcare book.

I'd like you to consider Thom Nickels' *Out in History* for that second shelf of books that, while not absolutely necessary, come really close. We know that coming out is a process that enriches us. We also know that reading a GLBT book for the first time is another step that propels you even further into the gay community. Reading Nickels' compendium of short but by no means small biographies of well-known homosexuals and fellow-followers is a third helpful, significant, and enriching step.

For the exacting among us, the title isn't precisely true. Not all of these people were "out" the way many of us are today. For one reason, some of them preceded the current gay movement said to have begun after the Stonewall Rebellion of 1969. What Michelangelo (page 90) Florence Nightingale (p 84), Frederick of Prussia (p 176), or George Sand (p 197) would have been like if any of them had lived today is anyone's guess. Mike, Flo,

Fred and "George" might have been even more popular than they were in their own time.

Another reason the title isn't perfectly accurate is that some of these people came from places and cultures where being gay was either unimportant or already accepted. The Native American, Sahaykwisa (p 194), comes to mind, as does Yukio Mishima (p 173), who fulfilled in his lifetime a Japanese standard set by gay warriors three centuries before. After all, "coming out" assumes being "in" in the first place.

Not all of these names will be familiar to you. A batch of them weren't to me and I pride myself on knowing my gay forebears. Try these on: Charles Stoddard (p 113) Marguerite Radclyffe-Hall (p 158) Nicholas Sension (p 182), Henry Gerber (p 200), Dr. Mary Walker (p 232), Carlton Willers (p 9), or David Norris (p 50). Well? See! Any book that can increase my knowledge like Thom Nickels' volume is a welcome addition to my library and I'll bet yours as well.

I've been privileged to meet some of these people in my life: Andy Warhol (p 6), Quentin Crisp (p 101), James Baldwin (p 122), James Merrill (p 133), Ned Rorem (p 142), Malcolm Boyd (p 152), Gore Vidal (p 164), Rainer-Werner Fassbinder (p 188), Robert Mapplethorpe (p 209), Paul Cadmus (p 214), John Rechy (p 220), Allen Ginsberg (p 244), William Burroughs (p 252), Susan Sontag (p 59), W.H. Auden and Chester Kallman (p 241). Some of them I've met more than once. Several of them I've known quickly but in depth. Others over extended periods of time, during which we had various "personal" conversations as well as other kinds of inter-relations. Even so, I learned something about each of them from this book that I'd not known before. Something telling, something important: yet another reason to read *Out in History*.

Then there are all those figures I'd known some-thing of, often very little beyond a name and maybe a fact about one of her/his actions—Hilda Doolittle, Harold Action, Valerie Solanas. After reading Nickels' portraits-in-miniaure I felt I knew them a great deal better.

Here's some of what I learned from *Out in History:*

Carlton Willers believes he was Andy Warhol's "only authentic boyfriend" even though they stopped seeing each other long before the artist became famous. To which I must ask: then who or what was Billy Name, the completely ubiquitious figure at Warhol's Factory, if not a boyfriend?

Composer/Memoirist Ned Rorem said that "music does not have a sexuality and sexuality cannot be de-fined muscially." Tell that to Bizet who wrote *Carmen,* or Verdi, whose Countess Eboli in *Don Carlo* and Duke of Mantua in *Rigoletto* ooze sexuality in a single short aria. Tell that to Richard Strauss who shows intercourse in the opening of *Der Rosenkavalier* and Act Two of *The Egyptian Helen.* And by the way, Ned and I disagreed several times.

Writers Joe Orton and his lover/flatmate Kenneth Halliwell "created their own personal theater in the de-facing of books fom the Islinginton Library. They'd steal art prints or cut out lewd photos and paste them inside books of etiquette, create false blurbs, or alter authors' bios. After the damage, Orton would then love to hide in the library and watch the shocked patron's reactions."
—For this vandalization the two men were imprisoned for six months!!!

Despite numerous and sometimes very public affairs with women, Susan Sontag never came out, and after her death opinions columns in major newspapers contended over the meaning of what Nickels calls her "hiding."

The philosopher George Santayana suffered a 40-year long, unconsummated love for Frank Rusell, elder brother of the controversial Betrand Russell. When Frank was imprisoned in 1880 for bigamy, a result of "excessive heterosexuality," Santayana consoled his loved one by letter. He also admitted in later years that, while Frank was a major part of his life, he was only a "bit-player" in Frank' s life. In sad fact, Frank Russell couldn't even remember Santayana's name and often called him "Sergeant."

The great British composer Benjmain Britten and his lover, tenor Peter Pears, pretended to have separate bedrooms when they were photographed for a popular magazine. And incidents of people scrawling the word "pansy" over posters announcing Britten-Pears recitals were common.

Nursing in 1847—when Flo Nightingale became a nurse—was not considered an honorable profession because it was seen as attracting prostitutes and drunkards. This is *nursing* we're talking about.

Harold Action's father, one of the wealthiest in England, "would humiliate him by locking the family villa whenever he believed his son was staying out late with young men. Action was forced to scale the masion walls like a delinquent intruder."

Then too, as found in Nickels' book, Susan Sontag, not known as particularly given to hyperbole, said of one gay writer—" He was our Sartre, our Camus, but he had gifts neither ever had: an intrepid feeling for what human life is about, a fastidiousness and a breadth of moral passion." Capote? Tennessee? Bowles? Give up guessing who? It was Paul Goodman.

Why are these facts important to me and why should they be important to you? For the same reason *Out in History* is, and should be seen as, significant. There's the easy and usual reasons of one-upmanship: "Geez, look at all the important queers. A lot more than the mere ten percent of us in the population allegedly allowed. Being gay must be pretty special in all ways! And thus *a lot better* than being straight." It's a cheap shot, yet still an effective one. And good for the ego.

A bit less vainglorious, a book like this contains inspiration. I know: a terrible word, a misused word, an overused word. But it actually says what it should here: by reading about these men and women, you can be literally "in-spired," meaning you have new breath brought into yourself. And we know that new breath leads to better mental and physical health.

I'm going to read *Out in History*, both portraits and interviews, often. I hope you will too, and encourage your circle to follow suit. Because then, we will have collectively increased the demand for Thom Nickels to write a second volume!

Felice Picano
Back House, April, 2005

INTRODUCTION
Then and Now

Walt Whitman and writer Bayard Taylor, two notable figures in 19th-century Philadelphia, stand as examples of what it was like to be gay or lesbian in an age far different than our own.

Whitman scarcely needs an introduction; yet, there are still people who insist that the poet was not really gay. However, Oscar Wilde's impression after spending some private time with Whitman should be granted full weight. When asked by George Ives in London whether the American poet was "one of the Greek Lovers," Wilde replied, "Of course, I have the kiss of Walt Whitman still on my lips." Then, of course, there was Edward Carpenter, a former Anglican priest who claimed to have slept with Whitman and that it was Whitman's belief, as well as his own, that the way to recharge an old body was to sleep next to a young man.

Bayard Taylor, born in Kennett Square, Pennsylvania, traveled throughout Europe in lieu of a university education. He began to write poetry, but first attracted notice when he wrote essays about his European travels for the (Philadelphia-based) *Saturday Evening Post*. Of course, being a man of his times, he became engaged to his high school sweetheart, Mary S. Agnew. The engagement, like all suspicious engagements, was a long one. What forced the marriage was Mary Agnew's coming down with tuberculosis. Taylor seemed to realize that he had little time to make an impression and, sure enough, the couple had only been married for two months when she died in December 1850.

Whitman's career was a hodgepodge of newspaper editorships that came and went. He was always getting into trouble or having personality conflicts and editorial clashes with higher-ups. Then there was his poetry — new, bold, homoerotic, and way over the Victorian "line." Taylor, on the other hand, played the journalism games and accordingly became "respected," even beloved.

When the 1876 centennial rolled around, Whitman and Taylor both applied to write the national centennial hymn. Whitman was hurt and jealous when Taylor was accorded the honor. Yet, Whitman biographer Jerome Loving wonders why the poet should have been surprised. Whitman's work was inciting some to label him "disgusting" and "vile," and Taylor himself called Whitman a "third-rate poet attempting to gratify his restless passion for personal notoriety." Taylor also condemned Whitman's repeated and unauthorized use of Ralph Waldo Emerson's congratulatory letter to the poet as a preface in various editions of *Leaves of Grass*. One time he even stated that Whitman's book was not fit to "be read aloud under the evening lamp."

Who knows what really motivated Taylor's attacks on the Camden poet? At the time, Taylor was a media darling, his fame worldwide; Whitman's impact, by contrast, lacked punch in the United States, although it was beginning to grow in Europe. Was all this merely jealous rivalry between two divas? It seems so. To his credit, Taylor was no prude; he just knew how to play the polite society game. His novel *Joseph and His Friend*, which was serialized in the *Atlantic Monthly*, was the first American gay novel. Taylor even dedicated the 1869 book to those "who believe in the truth and tenderness of a man's love for man, as of man's love for woman: who recognize the trouble which confused ideas of life and the lack of high and intelligent culture bring upon a great portion of our country population. To all such, no explanation of this volume is necessary. Others will not read it."

John W. M. Hallock, in *Homosexuality and the Fall of Fitz-Greene Halleck*, writes that Taylor's novel "was introduced by lines from a Shakespearean sonnet: 'The better angel is a man right fair'," and that "in spite of Coleridge's editing of pronouns in Shakespeare's sonnets, they have long served as a rich source for homosexual allusion."

Still, ask anyone in Kennett Square today if they know that Bayard Taylor was a gay man and you're likely to draw a blank. Nowhere is that fact mentioned in the 100th commemorative anniversary book by Joseph A. Lordi, *Our First Hundred Years, Bayard Taylor and Libraries in Kennett Square*. The closest Lordi comes to acknowledging Taylor's "differences" is when he describes the poet as feeling uncomfortable and unpopular in his hometown: "The neighborhood had always criticized Bayard Taylor, and he had quite refused to order his life and conduct by the canons, which were acceptable about him. Nor would he quietly go his own way and pay no attention to the criticism. It offended his sense of justice and of catholicity.... He was vexed and teased by the petty gossip which assailed him, and by the direct assaults upon his freedom."

Called "the most outspoken advocate of 'the other' [homosexual] love in mid-century America," Taylor, at the time of his death, had not only published some 50 books but also just been appointed ambassador to Germany.

Whitman, on the other hand, had to depend on the financial kindness of strangers. (As if his situation wasn't bleak enough, immediately following Whitman's death, Camden urchins broke into his wine cellar and stole all the champagne.) Yet Whitman is clearly better known today. His star has totally eclipsed the respected Kennett Square gentleman who, while truly great in his own right, restricted the light of truth to a contained glow under an evening lamp.

Being someone who is forever searching for good history books and biographies that will whet my appetite for delving into the lives of notable queers, when I stumbled upon Daniel Mark Epstein's book, *Lincoln and Whitman: Parallel Lives in Civil War Washington*, I sensed that I had found a gem.

A book devoted to the "relationship" between Lincoln and Whitman had to come along sooner or later. Whitman lovers know what the American president meant to the bard, namely by elegies such as "When Lilacs Last in the Dooryard Bloom'd" and the schoolboy poem, "O Captain! My Captain!" Biographies of Whitman, from Jerome Loving's tome to Justin Kaplan's work, have all referred to Whitman's fascination with, and love for, Abraham Lincoln, despite the fact that historians and students of history know that there was no real friendship or anything tangible between the two men. In fact, the closest they came to meeting was one Halloween night when Whitman happened to be in the White House to pick up a set of round-trip train tickets to New York so he could go home and vote in the 1863 elections. Lincoln's secretary, John Hay, handed Whitman the tickets as the poet caught a glimpse of Lincoln talking with a friend in an adjoining room. "...His face & manner have an expression...inexpressibly sweet—one hand on his friend's shoulder the other holding his hand," Whitman wrote of that moment.

Whitman and Lincoln had frequent distant eye-to-eye contact in Washington, a "relationship" that Epstein writes had "become a welcome and comforting fixture on the road to Lincoln's summer retreat."

But if the "relationship" between Whitman and Lincoln was ethereal, detached and in some respects a mystery, why a book subtitled *Parallel Lives*? The hope of course is that the author's promise of "parallel lives" will be culled from new insight, scholarship or recent revelations, such as Larry Kramer's insightful outing of Lincoln some years ago when he noted that between 1839 and 1842 Lincoln had an intense live-in friendship with his law clerk, Joshua Fry Speed. For a period of four years the two men slept together in the same bed and were as inseparable as Whitman's comrades in his poem, "We Two Boys Together Clinging." Speed, however, is granted only a fleeting reference in *Parallel Lives*: ["(Lincoln) once told his friend, Joshua Fry Speed: 'My mind is like a piece of steel—very hard to scratch anything on it, and almost impossible, after you get it there, to rub it out.'"] This is disappointing to say the least. A small notation on Kramer's research on Lincoln and Speed would have sufficed to acknowledge that something "really" parallel in their lives had occurred.

Lincoln and Whitman opens with Lincoln as a young lawyer reading a new book of poetry, *Leaves of Grass*, in his Springfield law office in 1857. Lincoln's law clerk at the time, Billy Herndon, a rabid collector of books, had bought a copy of *Leaves of Grass* after reading that Ralph Waldo Emerson called it "the most extraordinary piece of wit and wisdom that America has yet contributed." Herndon shared his copy with the future president. Later, Lincoln, with his long legs resting on the edge of his desk, couldn't put *Leaves of Grass* down, but when he brought the book home it barely managed to escape being burned.

Despite his family's "fiery" disapproval of Whitman, Lincoln was a truth seeker and not about to dismiss the poet's work as vulgar. After all, Lincoln was so homespun he once caused Herndon to remark that the young lawyer "never could see the harm in wearing a sack-coat instead of a swallowtail to an evening party, nor could he realize the offense of telling a vulgar yarn if a preacher happened to be present."

The book's curious interweave of biography, literary analysis and quaint, children's book-style storytelling gives the work an uneven quality. Yet, despite its bumpiness, the book never quite loses its charm. The biographical portrait of Boston abolitionist Charles Sumner ("His appearance was splendid, his vanity transparent...Sumner took pride in his long and shapely hands, especially their whiteness...."), as well as Sumner's meeting with Whitman, provides an interesting glimpse into the social politics of Washington at the time.

As a young Vietnam War-era conscientious objector living in Boston in 1971, I happened to rent a room in Sumner's old house on Beacon Hill's Hancock Street. My second-floor room could have been lifted straight out of the 19th century. The furnishings had a worn, antique quality, as if they'd not been changed since that time. A lone sink stood in the corner of the room (where Sumner washed and lotioned his hands, perchance?).

Beside the bed was an imposing and unforgettable armoire that was so old it surely must have stored Sumner's Washington wardrobe and white gloves. In those days I knew nothing about Sumner except that he had been a famous abolitionist. I certainly could not have known that he "took pride in his long and shapely hands, especially their whiteness."

Like Lincoln, Whitman, according to Epstein, was a man very out of touch when it came to clothing himself or mingling with Washington society. With his ragged clothes and Wild Buffalo Bill hats and jackets, no wonder he had doubts about the fastidious Sumner, who was so in love with his own hands that he would study them "as they rested upon his crossed knees."

Unlike Lincoln, however, Whitman finds gay love in Washington. There is Peter Doyle and a few others. (In one instance Whitman gives gifts to Thomas Sawyer, a soldier, and then invites him to his house, but is stood up. The tale has a contemporary ring: an older-than-middle-aged man vying for the affections of youth and making a fool of himself.)

In searching for connections between the historical and the contemporary, one has only to consider the case of Edward Hyde, also known as Lord Cornbury, the royal governor of New Jersey (1703-1708). Most historians agree that Lord Cornbury was a cross-dresser and a corrupt politician. Although his portrait (in a woman's evening gown) hangs in the New Jersey Historical Society, more people became aware of this fact after New Jersey Governor James McGreevey's resignation on August 12, 2004 (at which time he announced that he was gay and had an extra-marital affair with a man while in office). Certain websites with a right-wing bias seemed to take great delight in aligning the Governor to

Lord Cornbury's governorship in order to draw a correlation between homosexuality, corruption and cross-dressing. No evidence exists that Lord Cornbury was gay, of course, but among social reactionary types any man who wears a dress must be viewed as homosexual as overwhelming statistics indicating that most cross dressers are heterosexual are inevitably troubling to these thinkers in black and white.

In 1965, Arthur D. Pierce of the New Jersey Historical Society wrote: "Striding along the ramparts of Fort Anne in New York was a strange figure in feminine attire. Some believed rumors that it was Queen Anne herself: the gown, from a distance, seemed sufficiently resplendent. It was not the Queen, however. It was not even a woman. It was the first royal governor of New Jersey: Lord Cornbury, less elegantly known as Edward Hyde."

Pierce wrote that Cornbury's "parading undermined faith in royal rule from its very beginning," and that this had an adverse affect by encouraging "public habits and attitudes which eventually would lead to revolution."

In the 1700s the people of New Jersey were known as "Jarzies." The colony had a rambunctious reputation. Riots and clubbings were daily events and at one point there was what Pierce calls a "junior-size rebellion" in which "rowdy crowds brought that [Proprietary] government, for a time, to a virtual standstill."

Lord Cornbury, in his Queen Anne regalia, was the epitome of corruption; he was involved in a number of real estate schemes and there wasn't much he wouldn't do for money. When his wife died, he attended the funeral in women's clothing. Some people assumed that he dressed in drag because he was drunk or because he wanted to look more "royal." One writer at the time said that "half his time is spent [dressed] that way."

Countering the view that Cornbury scandalized everyone he met, gay historian Dick Leitsch wrote: "The European court probably didn't find Lord Cornbury as 'extraordinary' as the Colonials did since this was the great age of drag in Europe. Boys still played women's roles on stage and many boy actors were minions to royalty. Philip, Duke of Orleans and brother to Louis XIV, lived in drag, as did his follower, the Abbe de Choisy, a priest who served the French Ambassador to various other countries and who died 'a handsome dowager' only 10 years before Cornbury went to Hanover."

One historian, Patricia U. Bonomi of New York University, contends that the portrait purchased by the New York Historical Society in 1952 for $1,000 is not of Lord Cornbury but a masculine woman. Bonomi dates the portrait at 1867, one hundred years after Cornbury's death.

Whether fact or fable, however, Lord Cornbury, the famous "Jarzie" cross-dresser, has now been linked to the unfortunate misadventures of former Governor McGreevey.

Most gay men have known men like Governor Jim McGreevey, the closeted gay married man being a "type" in the gay world. Some marry women knowing they are gay but do it for family or societal reasons (Mom wants grandchildren; Enron may not want a gay CEO, etc., etc.). Other married gay men have no idea they are gay until a breakthrough occurs, but oftentimes by then they are years into their marriage. Others are bisexual and see sex with men as a purely mechanical endeavor. They may consider it "not cheating," since they reserve their emotional lives (and heart) for their wives.

There are the occasional open marriages where the husband is permitted to have a "boys' night out," as long as he keeps his priorities—family first—in order.

McGreevey falls into one of these categories. Judging by the serene attitude of his wife, Dina, during the August 2004 press conference, my hunch is that she knew he was gay and allowed him a certain degree of freedom in his personal life. The governor was then able to be himself to some extent, to be "seen" in certain places (like Atlantic City) with gay men or with companions that raised some eyebrows here and there. Rumors like this abounded for years. I first heard them years ago when a friend of mine said that a friend *of his* had spotted the governor in an Atlantic City casino with "an obvious boyfriend."

McGreevey married because that's what was expected of him in pursuing a viable political career. Given his (self-admitted) torturous state of mind regarding his sexuality, he could never have evolved into a crusading Barney Frank, for instance. When he offered his resignation after admitting to an adult consensual affair with another man, he said he was leaving office to spare others pain, mainly his elderly parents, who stood by him at the podium during his truth-telling press conference.

That pain, of course, would have come from the media. President Clinton was demonized by a media obsessed with his private sex life. Have you any doubt that the very same media would have torn Governor McGreevey to shreds had he stayed in office and fought Golan Cipil's almost certainly false charges of sexual harassment?

All you have to do is watch Robert Kane Pappas' documentary film, *Orwell Rolls in His Grave*, to see how American society is becoming a kind of oligarchy. The film documents how the mass media since the Reagan years has been brought under the control of a handful of American companies and how their one goal is to gain more control in reporting the news. The fact is; big media in the U.S. has aligned itself with the more radically conservative faction of the Republican Party. The result? Mass media has pushed the right wing agenda in order to gain political favor and fatten their coffers. This has created the new media we see today: the selfish Moloch that conspired to "eat" President Clinton, that reports some news stories and ignores others, that cancels a telemovie like *The Reagan's*. While corporate ownership affects every television venue to a greater or lesser degree, the empires known as Fox News and Clear Channel are two blatant examples of what George Orwell called "doublespeak."

Governor McGreevey didn't want his family torn to shred by this machine, so he bowed out. Even had Democratic bosses pressured him into resigning, they're doing so undoubtedly hinged on the "media-eating" aspect as well.

On the day of McGreevey's resignation, homophobes and social conservatives had a field day in AOL chat rooms (fast becoming the internet equivalent of Fox News). Most said it was a great day for America. They were referring to McGreevey's downfall and the fact that the California Supreme Court had nullified the 4,000 same-sex marriages preformed in San Francisco around that time. Some Internet yahoos stated that McGreevey broke the law — the law in this case being the law against adultery. These yahoos casually assumed that America has already broken down what remains of the barrier between church and state, and that the country is firmly in the hands of the Christian fundamentalist Taliban.

But let's move onto Golan Cipil.

For beginners, he reminds me of Andrew Cunanan, the man who shot Versace.

Other than that, it's easy to see that he was a sexual opportunist and gigolo who knew how to say 'Yes' when it was financially advantageous for him to do so. Straight? Well, if by *straight* you mean someone who doesn't kiss or take too active a role, then I guess he was straight. But don't tell me he was *coerced* into having sex with Jim McGreevey! Someone like this obviously enjoys power, and a Marquis de Sade-like situation in which he was able to wield power over a United States governor must have been an especially delicious erotic thrill.

Was it wrong for McGreevey to put Cipil on the state payroll? You bet. Was it an "impeachable" offense? No way. Should the governor have resigned? Not on your life.

Cipil states that the Governor "made repeated sexual advances," and charges him with sexual harassment but given McGreevey's temperament—balanced and hardly 'Metallica macho'—I think it's doubtful that the Governor bulldozed Cipil or kept hitting on him a la *Fatal Attraction*. The governor may have used the art of gentle persuasion when his love relationship with Cipil cooled; he may even have attempted to woo the estranged Cipil without untoward arm-twisting. This is clearly not sexual harassment, but Cipil, the consummate opportunist, besides feeling squeezed out of a state job, saw an opportunity to make money.

Recently I spoke with someone who works in the Trenton state house who is a casual acquaintance of the governor. "X" told me that he knew McGreevey when he was a New Jersey Assemblyman and that he'd had a feeling then that he was gay. "He seemed entirely alone and in need of gay friends. He's such a kind person and so full of humor. He's the sort of guy who comes up to you with a smile and a hug. He would have done anything for anybody. That's why I think he latched onto this Cipil guy. He had to find love wherever he could, on a catch-as-catch-can basis. And Cipil took advantage of that and his good nature. I've no doubt that Jim wanted to help him. He should not have resigned. Too bad he didn't stay and fight."

At any rate, McGreevey's "fall from grace" was certainly one of the more dramatic "outings" in gay American history.

One familiar truth prevalent in many of the lives described in these essays is the power that religion has exercised in setting the foundation for homophobia. Name any queer, famous or not, and all you have to do is trace whatever discrimination he or she encountered in life to the threshold of religion. As Bishop John Spong once told me: "Those conservatives don't want to hear that homosexuals are not abnormal children of the devil—something the church in the 16th century branded left-handed people."

Spong, of course, knows that there are lots of reasons why the Church ought to be hated. "The church has burned so many homosexuals throughout history that the little sticks used to start the fires (i.e. faggot) became identified with the victims. In the western Catholic tradition, women have been called sub-human and have been told the only way they can be saved is if they have babies or become a nun. You see; if you're the victim of the religious establishment, it's hard to love it."

FIFTEEN MINUTES OF FAME

Writer Victor Bockris is standing at the podium at Moore College in Philadelphia. He's in Philly as part of a "Silent Cinema" series at Moore and has just introduced Andy Warhol's 1964 film, *Kitchen*, starring Edie Sedgwick.

The crowd is hip/artsy. Straight couples predominate: skinny blond girls with '20s "flapper" hairstyles, their lean, pale boyfriends with conspicuous sideburns. I'm crammed beside a fidgety Asian student, about 20, who looks like an engineering whiz. Considering the bisexual nature of *Kitchen*'s cast of characters, I can't help but imagine that most of the boys and girls in the audience have had at least one homosexual experience.

Kitchen is a disaster, of course. Norman Mailer once called it a "descent into the hell of boredom." The 'story' takes place in the kitchen of a New York apartment and is reflective, one is to presume, of Warhol's perception that life is pretty much a compendium of mundane chores, ennui, and pointless chatter.

The Asian kids flees after twenty minutes of watching Edie put on her makeup as her male roommate washes dishes with a detergent called "Trend."

After the film has ended, Bockris asks the crowd: "So. What did you think?" For a second there's absolute quiet. Then Bockris blurts what is on everyone's mind: "Terrible, right!" going on to explain that *Kitchen* is one of those films that must be seen in order to understand Warhol's genesis as a film maker, how he eventually came to make such films as *Heat, Trash,* and *Lonesome Cowboys.*

Twenty-four hours later, I'm sitting with Bockris on the patio of a house in West Philly. I tell him I'm finally able to put a face to the name. Years ago we both wrote for *The Distant Drummer,* Philly's only underground newspaper. Bockris was already in New York, working at Warhol's Factory. (His book, *The Life and Death of Andy Warhol* was published in 1989. He has also written biographies of William Burroughs, Patti Smith and John Kale of the Velvet Underground.)

Talking to Bockris is like watching a film of New York in the seventies. He mentions dinner parties with William Burroughs, Mick Jagger and Andy. Or how he introduced writer Christopher Isherwood to Burroughs when he brought Isherwood to Burroughs' bunker. Or how he saw Andy at the Factory sitting alone in the dark in a depressed slump because his friend, Lou Reed, did not invite him to his wedding. Or how Andy used to come to Philadelphia on weekends to visit Henry McIlhenny at his mansion on Rittenhouse Square, or shoot film footage on the roof deck of another wealthy Philadelphian's house near 15th and Spruce. Or how Andy's Institute of Contemporary Art exhibit in Philadelphia marked the beginning of his career as a pop star, with hundreds of groupies waiting to see the King in his white wig, solar sunglasses and necklace of safety pins. Or how Andy, albeit fame and success, felt that he was a failure because he never had a sustaining love relationship (Allen Ginsberg and Burroughs felt similarly, Bockris insists).

Bockris mentions the time that Muhammad Ali gave Andy the cold shoulder (with Bockris acting as go-between) during a picture-taking session in Ali's Pennsylvania training cabin, the fighter brandishing his Islamic, self-righteous attitude and finally letting Andy have it with a forty-five minute diatribe about the decline of western morals as evidenced by pictures of two men fucking on newsstand magazine covers.

" '...That's so funny; I think he's a male chauvinist pig, right? He's a male chauvinist pig? Because, I mean, how can he preach like that? It's so crazy,' " Bockris quotes Andy as saying to him at the conclusion of Ali's tirade.

Bockris, who is straight, corrects me when I imply that Andy wasn't much of a gay activist. "Warhol was a militant homosexual. Absolutely. If you said *anything* negative about homosexuality, you were physically thrown out of the Factory—like, in a minute—taken by the arm, and pushed out the door. Oh, he was militant!"

Bockris says that as early as '62 or '63 Warhol was pushing his sexuality on people at a time when it was dangerous to be gay. "I mean, it could destroy your career." He mentions artist Jasper Johns who once denied that he was gay and who even went out of his way to "act macho."

Charades like that pissed Warhol off, he said.

"Warhol affected his gayness with his voice, with the way he behaved—all to upset people."

According to Bockris, what gave Warhol the courage to be open were the changes brought about by WWII. Men fighting together in foxholes and saving each other's lives knew everything about their fellow soldiers. If a gay man saved your life, his gayness became irrelevant. "There were a lot of gay people in the Army in those days. So after the war, in '45 or '50, before the cold war and the McCarthy era, there was a real openness in the culture. Andy, who went to college from '45-'49, interfaced with a lot of guys who had been to Europe and who were gay. They were like...macho guys strutting around campus, only they were gay and people *knew* they were gay, but nobody cared. That's how Andy became encouraged to open up to his gayness. By the time he came to New York in '49 the gay underground was fantastic. I met a lot of those guys involved in that...they had a wonderful time because they knew they were a new breed, a new group of people."

Unfortunately, that freedom of expression did not last and life for gays in the '50s and 60's, at least "above ground" was no Walt Disney frolic.

"It was a time when being gay was like death—you were totally dismissed," Bockris confirms. "I mean, you couldn't even invite people to dinner who were gay. People just didn't want to be with them. It wasn't until '74 or '75 that things changed."

Bockris goes on to say that he was heavily involved with gay people at that time. "...I was smack dab in the center of that gay world, which was by far the most exciting, brilliant, attractive and intelligent world that existed in New York or anywhere else."

The eighties saw another change. With the advent of AIDS, Bockris says that the gay people of New York closed off. "Things became separated because people were fighting for their lives. And everyone was suspect in some way. And I suddenly found myself not quite as welcome inside small social groups, which was upsetting."

Does Bockris think that Andy would fit in with today's culture?

"Today, everyone has retreated back into their groups. 'I'm this. You're that. We're separate.' and I think that's a great pity. The religious right has really taken over the culture. It's a very different kind of culture now..."

One that, Bockris insists, Andy, with his love of cross-referencing different types of people, would not like at all.

ANDY WARHOL

During the sixties and seventies, when the John Wayne mentality still ruled Middle America, films like *The Chelsea Girls*, *Women in Revolt*, *My Hustler*, *Trash*, *Lonesome Cowboys* and *Flesh* revolutionized American culture, influencing filmmakers like John Waters with their startling gay and bisexual images. *Lonesome Cowboys*, for instance, championed sex role reversals by featuring hunky cowboys who wore mascara. *My Hustler* dealt with male prostitution. *Trash* starred transvestite Holly Woodlawn. The masterminds behind these films were Paul Morrissey and Andy Warhol.

"Warhol," says artist Richard Serra in Victor Bockris' 1989 biography of Warhol, "occupied the captain's table at Max's Kansas City (a New York restaurant). He was already a historical figure. His people were making up their own tradition and it freed all of us. Everybody understood that he was right on the edge completely awake."

In Paul E. Cohen's Warhol documentary, we see the Warhola family after the death of the artist in 1987. On screen are old Byzantine Catholic ladies wearing spectacles, (fondly) recalling Andy's childhood. We see Andy's brother, John, in a green work shirt, worlds apart from the Pied Piper of New York's underground, "a man who makes people superstars of New York and then drops them," as poet Gregory Corso would later charge.

Born Andrew Warhola in Pittsburgh, Pennsylvania on August 6, 1928, Andy was the second son of Ondrej and Julia Warhola, both of whom had immigrated to America from Czechoslovakia. Andy's father was an arch-disciplinarian with a huge appetite for work, his childhood and youth having been spent in dire poverty. "I had three nervous breakdowns as a kid," Andy would write in his book, *The Philosophy of Andy Warhol*.

After his graduation from the Carnegie Institute in Pittsburgh in 1949, he moved to New York and found work as a commercial artist. His shoe designs brought him work in the art department of the I. Miller shoe store. He became so successful that within a year of his arrival there, he was able to purchase a townhouse on upper Lexington Avenue, which he later shared with his mother. In the mid-fifties he changed his name to Warhol.

In 1962, exhibitions of Warhol's Campbell's Soup can silk-screens were staged in New York and Los Angeles. The exhibition made Warhol world famous, and his reputation grew with tremendous speed so that by the mid-1960s he was the most famous plastic artist in the world.

Warhol's diary, published after his death, documents the darker side of people like Lee Radziwill, Jacqueline Onassis, Lou Reed, Truman Capote, Calvin Klein, Mick Jagger, Jerry Hall and Muhammad Ali. The diary detailed behind-the-scenes events in Warhol's studio (or "the Factory"), the attempt on his life by Valerie Solanas as well as his problems with boyfriend Jon Gould, who later died of AIDS. "The atmosphere at the Factory," writes Bockris, "resembled more than ever that of a feudal court. By the time of the king's arrival around noon, the waiting room was full of petitioners — minions waiting for his instructions or encouragement."

Although surrounded by superstar wannabes and groupies of both sexes, Warhol never let the party life that surrounded Studio 54 and the Factory drug culture impede his work. He attended mass every Sunday like a bourgeois car salesman and his life, overall, had an ascetic slant to it, protecting him from the disasters that befell many of his contemporaries.

As Fran Lebowitz said during the auction of his collection of art and antiques, "Andy must be so furious that he is dead."

Andy Warhol's First Boyfriend
CARLTON WILLERS

I first heard the name Carlton Willers while interviewing author Victor Bockris, when Bockris was in town to introduce an early (and bad) Andy Warhol film entitled *Kitchen*. Willers, Bockris told me, was Andy's first boyfriend and lover, and not only that, he lived right here in Philadelphia. A few days later I found Willers' name in the white pages and called him to introduce myself. I didn't know it at the time but I'd be calling Willers more than a year later when I signed a book contract to write and compile *Gay and Lesbian Philadelphia*, (published in 2002). Since I have always been a fan of Warhol's—I've read his diaries, several biographies, and even have an initialed (AW) serigraph hanging on my living room wall—I wanted a photograph and some comments from Willers for my book.

Willers, who has given many interviews to writers and authors over the years, told me that he had just turned down a request for an interview "from yet another Warhol biographer." Everything that can be said has already been said, he told me (Willers wouldn't tell me who the New York writer was, but I wonder if perhaps it wasn't Warhol biographer, Wayne Kostenbaum). Willers liked the fact that I was a Philadelphian, and the fact that my book would contain lots of photographs intrigued him. Willers, an avid collector of photographs himself who used to run a small New York art gallery, owns a first-class collection of photographs the University of Iowa published as a special book in 1996.

Talking with the lean and elegant Willers, I tried to imagine what Andy saw so many years ago when the two met in the New York Public Library when Willers, just 20 years old, was working as the secretary for the curator in the picture collection. Andy used to come to the library all the time to borrow photographs for his work. "Lots of artists came in there. Andy was one of them and that's how I met him," Willers told me. "One day he came up to me and said, 'You wanna go on a picnic with some people in Central Park?'"

The year was 1953. After the picnic Willers says that he went to Andy's apartment almost every evening.

"I often stayed there because Andy would work all night. He was doing ad work in those days and making lots of money doing it. There weren't that many galleries then. It was a lot of fun for me and I helped him with a lot of that, as did a lot of people. He loved to go out to the theater. He would never go alone and I would always go with him. He liked the wonderful musicals of the 1950s. It was a lot of fun for me, a kid from Iowa, who entered the Air Force, then went straight to New York. Andy was a lot of fun in those days. He was playful."

In those days Andy was living in a top floor apartment with his mother, Julia. Willers remembers Julia as being extremely funny and kind. He says that everybody loved her because she was even more playful than Andy. "She was innocent and spoke this broken English and was always taking care of Andy. She was this old Czech lady. She was as funny as Andy and she loved to laugh at funny things. Andy had many cats then, eighteen of them. They were all named Sam. Some of them were inbred and many of them were getting a little queer; they were cross-eyed, some of them. In those days Andy had a mess of stuff around him. There was always paper and art work because he was busy doing advertising, and the cats would come along and knock over whole bottles of India ink, but Andy never got upset. Then his mother would come in with this big bucket and mop—she just looked like a Czech chore woman. She had her bedroom in the back and she'd go to her Catholic church every Sunday."

Willers says that Julia would cook, though she'd never eat with him and Andy. "She was always very nice to me but the only time Andy and me had any time together was late at night after she had gone to bed and fallen asleep in the bedroom in the back. She also called me Andy's boyfriend. To her a boyfriend was just a chum. To her I was just staying over because I was helping him with his work. She was special because I don't think she understood much about Andy's world. I don't think she understood they gay thing at all."

Julia, of course, had just come to New York one day on a visit and never left. She also kept trying to get Andy interested in girls. "Andy thought this was hilarious. Sometimes people would come to his studio and she'd see them and point out a girl and say, 'Andy, why don't you get married to her?'

"Andy's ad drawings were very elegant and beautiful in those days and everyone knew it. Here's this little boy—he really was like a boy in those days with his cap on...literally, his shoe laces would always be broken and his tie would be askew but he'd walk into the Bonwit and Teller Ad Department and everybody loved him. He already had an image of himself, a persona. He always had a persona."

Willers believes that he was Andy's only authentic boyfriend. "He was kind of asexual but gay. He didn't have a gay life so to speak though he had a thing about beautiful people and he loved beautiful boys. I think he might have intimidated people—I wasn't. I saw there was no line there. I just went right across it and I think he was very touched by it in a way. He was certainly not passionate. He was more passionate about food and eating. He loved going to certain restaurants where he liked the people. The reason that I had no trouble was that he was so self -conscious and with a lot of people he would sort of stand off and not cross that line. I think he loved having me there every night because otherwise he was alone with his mother."

Willers says that once in a while, while cuddling, Andy would cry. "This would usually come unexpectedly or spontaneously about something in his past that was sad. And he did have a somewhat sad past. They were very poor. His mother was always kind to him though. He was her favorite."

Sometimes when Willers was with Andy there would be mild arguments but these happened when friends of Andy's would say, "Let's go to this party," and Andy would say no because he would not like somebody who was going to be there. "I knew a lot of people thought, 'Well, we all want to go to this party so why can't we go?'" Willers says.

Andy was obsessed with becoming famous and he'd often say, "Gee, I wish I could be famous," though Willers doesn't think that Andy ever thought he'd become as famous as he did.

He was also insecure about his looks. "I thought he was much too self-conscious. He hated being bald and his tendency to put on weight. He liked sweets a lot. Often after he was out running around the town he'd buy all these voluptuous cakes and pastries and he liked ice cream, and that got him through the night sometimes." To hide his baldness Andy wore caps in the 1950s. "He wouldn't take the cap off," Willers says. "We'd go to rather nice dinner parties with rather nice prestigious people and he wouldn't take his hat off. He wouldn't even take his cap off in the theater. One day I said, 'Andy, why don't you get a hairpiece or something?' He actually did. He went to some place and got a very nice, well-matched hairpiece. He looked great in it. It looked like his real hair. Later, as his hair got completely white, he started going for white hairpieces."

Willers says that when he started Columbia he didn't see Andy on a regular basis, that he was too busy studying and working. When he finished Columbia he was offered a teaching job at Carnegie Tech, Andy's old alma mater. "Andy was intrigued by this. When I went out there I'd get cards from him and I'd visit him when I visited New York."

But something had changed. Andy was no longer the little blond boy with untied shoelaces walking around with his ad drawings, but had taken up with a film crowd and was now dressing in leather. "He remade himself. He didn't really look good in leather. He was a totally different person. People like myself or people who had known him before didn't know how to treat him because he wasn't the old Andy. They realized they were part of Andy's old world and not a part of the new world. It didn't bother me. He was starting to get famous for his pop art work and then started to make these films. The film people changed him. He almost didn't want to recognize you in the street when he ran into you. That happened to me several times but it truly didn't bother me because I didn't want to be in that world anyway. I knew that *he* had to be in that world. But I still ran into him from time to time when he wasn't with those people and he was still the same old Andy."

After this, Willers says, the wigs got crazier and crazier.

When Willers moved back to New York and opened a small art gallery, Andy came to visit from time to time. Willers would also run into him a lot at auctions. "He would often be alone, buying art. That's when I would run into him and we would talk and he was very much the same."

When Andy died, Willers was invited to the private memorial mass at St. Patrick's cathedral but opted not to go. He wasn't ready for all the hoopla. "Once you get to a certain point," he says, talking about Andy's fame, "it feeds on itself and it gets bigger and bigger. Andy didn't deal well with this towards the end of his life. He tried to keep up this persona. Had he lived to be old, where would that have gone? How could he finally take off these masks and be himself again? This would have been very difficult...everybody wanted him to be Andy Warhol. I think this happens to people who become famous and some people deal with it well and some don't."

VALERIE SOLANAS
The Radical Lesbian
Who Shot Andy Warhol

The book, *SCUM Manifesto* by Valerie Solanas, opened my eyes to yet another part of the Warhol saga.

...Valerie Solanas, an angry woman (and lesbian), shoots Andy Warhol in 1968. All hell breaks loose. News of the attempted assassination gets buried deep within the pages of The New York Times, preempted by the latest on the New York City garbage strike. Meanwhile, Warhol almost gives up the ghost, as Solanas is booked on attempted murder and illegal possession of a gun. She's sent packing to a psychiatric hospital.

End of story? Not quite.

Nobody expected Warhol's penchant for using people to erupt in bloodshed, but once Ms. *Solanas* felt used and abandoned by the King of Pop Art, the sinister die was cast. Solanas, who would eventually appear in Warhol's film, *I, A Man,* originally approached him with her play, *Up Your Ass,* hoping that he would produce it. Warhol, deeply involved with other projects, glanced at the manuscript and, commenting on how *well typed* it was, promised Solanas that he would read the work.

After waiting what she considered long enough for a response, Solanas contacted Warhol, only to be told that he'd lost the manuscript. From that point forward, he not only gave Solanas the runaround, but at one point even joked that she should work at the Factory as a typist. Enraged, the feminist retaliated with repeated and vociferous demands for money for her lost manuscript. Instead, Warhol paid her $25 to appear in *I, A Man*.

Had Warhol known that Solanas had just completed her *Society for Cutting Up Men Manifesto*, perhaps he would have made more of an effort to placate her. Even when Factory "superstar," Ultra Violet finally read the manifesto to him, Warhol failed to take to heart Solanas' proclamation that, "The male is, by his very nature, a leech, an emotional parasite and, therefore, not ethically entitled to live, as no one has the right to life at someone else's expense."

But then again, Warhol was not—by *Manifesto* definition at least—a Man, but a fag, and therefore not the enemy. For in Solanas' world, fags were automatic members of the Men's Auxiliary of SCUM. "...Faggots who, by their shimmering, flaming example, encourage other men to de-man themselves and thereby make themselves relatively inoffensive...." In other words, allies.

"The fag, who accepts his maleness, that is, his passivity and total sexuality, his femininity," Solanas wrote, "is also best served by women being truly female, as it would then be easier for him to be male, feminine."

After the shooting, Solanas was lionized by some. Radical feminist lawyer, Florynce Kennedy, called her "one of the most important spokeswomen of the feminist movement." The National Organization of

Women saw something valuable in Solanas' actions, and Ti-Grace Atkinson called Solanas the "first outstanding champion of women's rights." Norman Mailer jumped into the fray and referred to Solanas as "the Robespierre of feminism." Unfortunately for Warhol and Solanas, both eternally hungry publicity hounds, New York City's garbage strike stayed in the forefront of the news and Warhol's near-death experience became a small afterthought in the annals of Art News.

Avital Ronell's ultra-smart *SCUM Manifesto* introduction bristles with psychological insights, witty asides, and illuminating passages having to do with Solanas' peculiar but visionary take on all things cultural and male. Ronell compares Solanas to the Unabomber, Medusa, a girl Nietzsche, Lorena Bobbitt, and Medea. "There is no doubt that Solanas felt threatened by the Factory girls, painfully pitting her butch androgyny against the hyper-femininity that Warhol favored. She was one lonely lady in the heady glamour days of Candy Darling and Viva, way before the guerilla girls, Lesbian Avengers, Queer Nation, et al..."Ronell writes.

Ronell adds that Solanas arrived "too early or too late on every scene" and that nobody needed a "run-away Hothead Paisan," or a "comic strip lesbian avenger in the summer of '68," the era when Bobby Kennedy, Martin Luther King and Malcolm X were "being slaughtered."

Solanas, a psychology major in college, did doctoral work at the University of Minnesota, where she supported herself by working in the psych department's animal research laboratory. It would seem her penchant for splicing and mutation would prove an excellent template for the manifesto in which her view of Man is examined from every social, cultural and philosophical perspective.

"Man," she writes, "is egocentric, trapped within himself, incapable of empathizing or identifying with others." He's also "a half-dead, unresponsive lump," and "trapped in a twilight zone halfway between humans and apes." Males are also obsessed with screwing, she postulates. "He'll swim through a river of snot, wade nostril-deep through a mile of vomit, if he thinks they'll be a friendly pussy awaiting him." As Solanas sees it, because Man hates his passivity, he projects it onto women, then proceeds to prove that he "is a Man."

Penis envy? Forget it. Men have pussy envy, which, according to Solanas, means that when Man accepts his passivity, defines himself as a woman, "and becomes a transvestite, he loses his desire to screw."

The manifesto is replete with generalizations, funny absurdities, truths, myriad convolutions, and visionary asides. Her prediction about how science will change humanity—minus the male baiting—has proven to be true: "When genetic control is possible—and soon it will be—it goes without saying that we should produce only whole, complete beings, not physical defects or deficiencies, including emotional deficiencies, such as maleness...." When Solanas died, penniless and alone, at a San Francisco welfare hospital in 1988 from emphysema and pneumonia, genetic engineering was still science fiction. These half-gems catch the reader by surprise, such as when Solanas writes, "The purpose of 'higher' education is not to educate but to exclude as many as possible from the various professions."

Is it true that men are roadblocks on the road to progress because of their inability to cooperate? Solanas believes that "Men cannot cooperate to achieve a common end, because each man's end is all the pussy for himself." She believes that men fail because they cannot tolerate different-ness in other men, which is threatening to them. Such tolerance might label them "fags whom he must at all costs avoid, so he tries to make sure that all other men conform." She sees men as being so insecure that their females must be Obvious Woman, "the opposite of Man, that is, the female must act like a faggot," aka Stepford Wife (Laura Bush, for example), Total Woman, drag queen.

There's more:

"If SCUM ever marches, it will be over the President's stupid, sickening face; if SCUM ever strikes, it will be in the dark with a six-inch blade."

"SCUM will couple-bust—barge into mixed (male-female) couples, wherever they are, and bust them up."

Suddenly morphing into the rational anthropologist, Solanas writes:

"In a sane society the male would not trot along obediently after the female. The male is docile and easily led, easily subjected to the domination of any female who cares to dominate him. The male, in fact, wants desperately to be led by females, wants Mama in charge."

Then it's back to Lorena Bobbitt: if SCUM took over the world she'd have men tell themselves over and over again, "I am a turd, a lowly abject turd."

Virginia Wolfe once cautioned that nothing should ever be written in anger. Had Solanas heeded this advice the more sensible parts of her argument might have helped influence a wider audience.

As it was, it was Warhol's extreme misfortune to have dubbed Solanas a "typist."

JEAN COCTEAU

When Jean Cocteau was born in 1889, his grandfather looked at him and said, "He's not at all ugly. In fact, he's a lovely little old man."

The "lovely little old man" would grow up to be a film writer, novelist, poet, director and draftsman, and a designer of posters, tapestries, stage sets, pottery, mosaics, chapels and costume jewelry. An international celebrity, Cocteau was also an opium addict who underwent frequent (and public) "cures" that were sensationalized by the press.

James Lord wrote in *Some Further Remarkable Men* that Cocteau "was forever worrying about his position, his influence, his popularity...there was next to nothing he shrank from doing to enhance all three..."

But Cocteau never compromised his homosexuality in order to elicit favors or privileges from mainstream heterosexual society. To the contrary, he was accepted by the social elite of his day because of his incredible wit and charm.

"Cocteau flaunted the deviant fate of his private life at a time when such license was still discountenanced by the authorities," observed Lord, a protégé and friend to Cocteau until the latter's death in 1963.

Even close friends such as Pablo Picasso were sometimes of two minds concerning Cocteau's sexuality. Enjoying Cocteau's company one moment, Picasso, a lifelong Communist, once said to Lord, "That buffoon...that perfidious arriviste, that vampire. How many young men do you think he's destroyed?"

While not generally homophobic, Picasso's attitude was influenced by Cocteau's opium addiction, a condition that afflicted most of his young lovers as well—the exception being the handsome actor Jean Marias whom Lord said was "the most sincerely devoted, beneficent, and altogether decent of any of them."

Cocteau's gift was his brilliant wit and his charming personality. Like Oscar Wilde, his best "work" in many ways was his conversational style—words never recorded on paper, but lost in thin air.

"Cocteau did all the talking, pausing only occasionally to allow somebody to argue with him, and thus provide a springboard towards a variation in the monologue," Lord wrote.

Cocteau's films, including *The Blood of a Poet* and *The Testament of Orpheus*, are noted for their classical and surrealist imagery, and are examples of what Lord calls Cocteau's greatest talents: his brilliant photographic impressions and his "prodigious mastery of rhetorical effects."

Cocteau wrote more than 50 plays, memoirs and poems, including *The White Paper*, a work of erotica. *The White Paper* is the story of a voyeur in a factory shower room who watches laborers bathe after a day's work. Commenting on his own homosexuality, the narrator says: "...I'm not willing just to be tolerated. That wounds my love of love and of liberty."

In his autobiography, *Professional Secrets*, Cocteau advises people to "cultivate whatever the public reproaches you for. That's you."

In Paris, Cocteau lived near the Palais Royal, and surrounded himself with antique and baroque objects he obtained in flea markets. He met 22-year old Edouard Dermit when he was 57; the attraction, according to Lord, was "instantaneous, like Hadrian beholding Antinous for the first time…" The relationship lasted 16 years.

Cocteau died in 1963 while recording a radio tribute to Edith Piaf.

JEAN GENET

He was an illegitimate, marginally educated child who spent his adolescence reading Mauriac, Gide and Dostoevsky while tending an old cow in the farmlands of central France. Former teachers recall a model altar boy who pretended to say mass for his friends' amusement, yet at sixteen wound up as an inmate at the prison at Mettray. His childhood was also marked by a refusal to engage in any kind of physical labor.

By the time of his death in 1986 from throat cancer, five years of Genet's life would be spent in jails. Petty theft constituted the bulk of his crimes, stealing rare books his primary obsession. Genet, who considered his role of thief more important than that of writer, stole from friends, even from the sculptor Giacommetti (the only man he genuinely respected). At the height of his fame, Genet's thievery became a game of sorts at social functions where nervous society matrons wondered what "terrible Jean" would pocket next.

His first novel, *Our Lady of the Flowers*, was written in jail on paper bags. When a guard destroyed the completed manuscript, he recreated the work from scratch. When Jean Cocteau championed this "new" descendant of Baudelaire and Rimbaud, Genet began calling Cocteau "Master" — what Andre Gide was to Genet several years before. (In time, Genet would come to find Cocteau superficial, "all flash," and Gide, who once rejected sections of Proust's *Remembrance of Things Past* for his magazine, 'Nouvelle Revue Francaise,' ultimately snubbed Genet, refusing to send him cash so the younger writer could act out Gide's earlier advice to "go out and experience life.")

Genet wrote all of his autobiographical novels within a seven-year period. Although he called his early works "jerk-off" fantasies, it troubled him that many regarded his works as pornographic. He did not want to be known as a pornographer and detested the later, salacious editions of his books. Even after Jean-Paul Sartre's canonization of him in "Saint Genet," and Genet's success as a playwright (*The Blacks*, *The Maids*, etc.), he was insecure about his status as a writer: "Am I really good?" he'd ask friends.

Early editions of his works were lavishly bound, resembling illuminated manuscripts. When rich French homosexuals ordered copies of these works, handsome boys would hand-deliver the privately printed editions.

Genet felt that a poet should work silently behind the scenes, but this changed for him when he met Sartre. Sartre called Genet and Thomas Mann "the greatest living writers," but Genet was "the greatest figure in French literature since Proust." Albert Camus, Sartre's close friend, so resented this evaluation that he refused to sign petitions seeking Genet's release from various prisons. Sartre's elevation of Genet almost paralyzed Genet.

In "Saint Genet," Sartre stated that Genet chose to be homosexual. Genet countered by saying that he had no more chosen homosexuality than he did the color of his eyes. In romantic matters, only once did the poet/playwright fall in love with another homosexual, Genet's predilection usually being straight-trade. He avoided socializing with other homosexuals; he even called them "prancing fags." He told Sartre that he never had sex with anybody he didn't feel a spark of love for, but a "spark" for Genet could last anywhere from five minutes to several years.

Genet, who championed the underdog and the despised of the world, aligned himself with the Black Panthers in the 1960s. He also supported the Palestine Liberation Organization. Greece was his favorite place in the world, a land where "the erotic charge is probably the most intense...It's the only country in the world where people were able to worship, honor their gods and also not give a damn about them."

BESSIE SMITH

Blues singer Bessie Smith was a woman-loving woman who faced oppression in the form of an abusive, playboy husband who beat her whenever he discovered her lesbian affairs.

Fortunately for Smith, her husband was illiterate, unable to understand what the gossip columnists were saying when they wrote about her love life, which bought her a little time between beatings.

"The Empress of the Blues," as she came to be called, always swore her lesbian lovers to secrecy. Fear motivated these private paths, because her husband, Jack Gee, stalked her everywhere. Smith was afraid of Gee, as were most of the women in her musical troupe, The Harlem Frolics. The obsessive Gee would track her down and punch her out—be it backstage or in a bar.

Smith once asked a bartender if she could hide from Gee by drinking in the ladies' room.

"It worked until the day he caught her coming out, and knocked her down in front of everybody," writes Chris Albertson, author of *Bessie*.

Born in 1898 in Tennessee, Smith met Gee in 1922 in Philadelphia when her career was beginning to take shape. (She'd already been divorced from Mark Love.)

Gee and Smith married in 1923. Three years later, she met Ma Rainey, "The Mother of the Blues."

"Legend has it that Ma Rainey literally kidnapped Bessie, that she and her husband forced the girl to tour with their show, teaching her in the process how to sing the blues," Albertson writes.

For a time, rumor had it that Rainey was the one who initiated Smith into lesbianism. Whatever the source, by 1926, Smith was pursuing Lillian Simpson, a novice chorus girl whom Smith taught to dance, and later invited to join her company, which already included female impersonators and lesbians.

"Lesbianism was accepted in The Harlem Frolics, and Bessie's fellow musicians were not shocked when she began sleeping with Lillian, but worried about her husband's reaction when he returned." Albertson writes.

Although Simpson and Smith's relationship was a stormy affair, the two remained lovers until Gee's threats of physical violence caused Simpson to desert Smith in Detroit. Smith, not one to belabor any personal sorrow, sought relief in a Detroit "buffet flat," a speakeasy of sorts that featured erotic shows and live sex acts of every imaginable type.

For a time, "The Empress of the Blues," lived on Kater Street in Philadelphia, an association that helped her earn the title "Philadelphia's Favorite Daughter."

Because Columbia Records' line of recordings for black artists—called "race records"—didn't consider racy themes or homosexuality as taboo, Smith was able to write "Soft Pedal Blues" for the female owner of the Detroit flat, as well as pen a number of gay and lesbian-themed songs, including "The Boy in the Boat," "It's Dirty But Good," and "Foolish Man Blues."

While traveling through Mississippi in 1937, the car in which Smith was riding collided with a truck. The accident almost severed Smith's right arm, and caused massive internal injuries. Albertson blames Smith's death on the delay in calling an ambulance, and not, as some have suggested, on the refusal of a white hospital to admit her as a patient.

ANDRÉ GIDE

André Gide lived for his art. Born to a wealthy family, as a young writer he had no financial worries and could afford to be experimental in his writing. For a brief time he associated himself with poet Stephane Mallarmé and the Symbolist School. Later, his affiliation with the Communist party and his brief attraction to Christianity were both heightened and terminated by his aesthetic sensibility. Indeed, throughout his life, Gide stopped short of any ideological commitment, remaining a firm believer in the life of the senses.

Many critics view Gide as the greatest journalist of the 20th century, but Gide himself believed that he was preparing for a "much greater work" (as a child he wondered if adults could see this "future great work" in his eyes). Because it is said that Gide's manor house in Normandy contained staircases that glowed like "polished amber," I shall apply that description to Benjamin Ivy's first-ever English translation of this little-known Gide work, *Judge Not*, which adds significantly to the Gide corpus.

Ivy, the author of biographies of Francis Poulenc, Arthur Rimbaud, and Maurice Ravel, has translated and written a lengthy introduction to a small book that's a testament to Gide's fascination and even obsession with crime and punishment. In novels such as *Lafcadio's Adventures,* Gide often explored the criminal mentality as well as the criminal's place in society. In *Judge Not,* Gide recorded his impressions and analyses of judicial cases while serving as a juror. He wrote about the cases in depth, examining both the facts of the case and the background of the accused in a way that dovetailed with his lifelong rejection of traditional morality. Many of the cases involved murder with adolescents as the accused, and one can imagine Gide using them as the raw material for his fiction. Although Gide declared that his writings on judicial cases were not "literature," they are nevertheless artful journalism in which Gide often saw facts that judges and jurors overlooked. As Ivy explains, although some critics have deemed *Judge Not* too graphic in its descriptions of violent crime, such charges appear illogical given the book's subject matter.

Gide used criminals in his fiction in order to explore human psychology. He himself was often considered an outcast or criminal because of his open defense of homosexuality in his writings — Jean Genet once referred to him as "the master" — and because of his brief alliance with the Communist Party. (Gide mourned what happened to Marxism twenty years after the Russian Revolution and documented these changes in *Return from the USSR.*) Despite his lifelong love of the Bible, he had a persistent wish to escape conventional morality and explore the sensual life. Writing about his youth in his journal in March 1893, he wrote: "I have lived until the age of 23 completely virgin and utterly depraved; crazed to such a point that eventually I came to look everywhere for some bit of flesh on which to press my lips." Although he married in 1895, the marriage ended once he announced his homosexuality. No longer content to live life according to values that were not his own, Gide advocated in *Fruits of the Earth* (1897) that one should partake of life's sensual pleasures rather than think of everything in terms of "sin."

The newly liberated Gide was proud of his emerging "new self." His reinvention of himself laid the groundwork for the private publication, in 1911, of *Corydon*, his masterful defense of homosexuality as expressed in the "homosexual models" of ancient Greece. The first edition was a mere twelve copies; later it would go on to 66 editions, representing 33,000 copies. Wrote Gide in *Corydon*:

"You must also recognize the fact that homosexual periods, if I dare use the expression, are in no way periods of decadence. On the contrary, I do not think it would be inaccurate to say that the great periods when art flourished—the Greeks at the time of Pericles, the Romans in the century of Augustus, the English at the time of Shakespeare, the Italians at the time of the Renaissance, the French during the Renaissance and again under Louis XIII, the Persians at the time of Hafiz, etc., were the very times when homosexuality experienced itself most openly, and I would even say, officially. I would almost go so far to say that periods and countries without homosexuality are periods and countries without art."

Gide considered *Corydon* his most important work. He remarked that he was awarded the Nobel Prize in 1947 *despite* this book.

In 1924 he published another controversial work that dealt explicitly with his homosexuality, the memoir *If It Die*, wherein he described his first homosexual experiences, his first attempt at authorship, and his family relationships. It was the openly homosexual content of this work that turned Gide into an international target of derision by some critics. (The American author Dashiel Hammet, on hearing that Gide admired his detective stories, said, "I wish that fag would take me out of his mouth!") Even as early as 1912 Gide was aggressively supporting the idea of homosexual rights, if only in his private writings. In a Journal entry, Gide wrote:

"At Calvi (near Corsica), the entire male population, young and older, prostitutes itself. Yet that's not quite the word, for it seems to be not so much a matter of money as of pleasure. Women are closely guarded, unapproachable; a girl is compromised if a young man speaks to her. ...In the dance halls men only dance with each other—and in a very sensual way. The little boys, from the age of eight, witness the sexual activities of their older brothers with the strangers they take down to the beach."

By today's standards, Gide might be labeled a compulsive cruiser: he often thought of his liaisons with boys as "loathsome." As a writer, however, he was entirely dedicated to his art, using every personal experience as fodder for his novels, which some critics maintained were nothing more than Gide's thinly veiled life experiences. The Vatican newspaper, *L'Osservatore Romano*, wrote in 1952 that, because of Gide (and especially *Corydon*), "things which until now would have been whispered in the era among adults have become something to boast of—to boast of indecently— among adolescents."

David Littlejohn writes in *The André Gide Reader* that "many of the attacks of this period were little more than vulgar, malicious gossip about Gide's character and habits. ...The usual innuendo, of course, behind the 'corruption of youth' label was that the fifty-to sixty-year-old Gide was seducing young lads into sexual perversion." Always the survivor, Gide, who had alienated both conservative moralists with his philosophy of the senses and the European Left with his criticism of the Soviet Union, experienced a rebound of sorts after publishing his *Journals* and winning the Nobel Prize for Literature in 1947.

Gide was almost sixty when he wrote *Judge Not*. Ivy attributes his fascination with crime and abnormality to his own sex life as a pederast at a time when homosexuality was still illegal and severely punished — which did not prevent him from engaging in it. It was only his personal fortune and his fame as a writer that shielded Gide from trouble with authorities. He knew that pursuing his object of desire — teenage boys — rendered him a criminal in the eyes of the law. He was continually on the prowl for fifteen-year-old boys in cinemas, trains, and the countryside, but was never arrested for these activities. Gide himself maintained that he avoided arrest by observing a potential sexual partner closely and by using a "deft approach" to seduction. One has only to read Alan Sheridan's *André Gide, A Life in the Present*, to learn about the risks the staid author of *Strait Is the Gate* was willing to take with young boys, many of whom he wound up fondling in public.

Gide never turned down jury duty and he even advised other writers to take time out to do likewise. Now, the jury system in France differs from the American system. For example, jurors may speak out and ask the court to put certain questions to a defendant or witness. With this rule in mind, Gide wondered, "Did I dare use this prerogative? It's hard to imagine how unsettling it is to rise up and speak in front of the court. If I ever had to 'testify,' I would surely lose my composure, and what would I feel in the defendant's box." But that does not seem to have been the case, as recorded in *Judge Not*. Gide was often appointed foreman because of his professional literary stature and patrician manner, and when he spoke to the president he did so eloquently and without much fanfare.

"Does an innocent man sound more eloquent and less disturbed than a guilty one? Nonsense!" Gide wrote. "As soon as he feels that he isn't believed, he might be even more disturbed since he is less guilty. He'll overdo his statements, his protests will seem more and more disagreeable, and he will be out of his depth." Gide was definitely in his depth as he took notes on case after case. What upset him most, he confessed, was the tendency among jurors, during serious cases when it was clear that the defendant was not guilty, to opt to punish the defendant anyway. "To these jurors, some punishment is necessary," wrote Gide, "so just in case, let's punish the man, since he's the one offered to us as a victim. But since we're not sure, let's at any rate not punish him too much."

Gide's attention to detail allowed him to see pertinent facts to which other jurors were blind. Consider the case of Charles, a 34-year old coachman, who allegedly stabbed his mistress, Juliette, to death. As witnessed by Juliette's landlady, the killing would appear to be a simple case of murder. And this was what the jury saw, despite the defense attorney's claim that Charles' act "was done without the idea of killing being quite specified in his mind." Gide considered the attorney's claim that the proof of this lay in the distribution of stab wounds and then posited: "Why didn't the defense attorney go further and say that, not only had Charles not wanted to kill, but that he dimly tried, while mutilating his victim, not to kill her and that, doubtless so as not to kill her, he had grabbed the knife just next to the blade, which is the only way that the stabbing could have been so intense yet cause such shallow wounds?" Fed up with the "appalling incompetence of jurors," Gide recorded how the jurors later changed their minds after a sentence of life imprisonment at hard labor was handed down. Stunned by the severity of the sentence, the jury chose to take another look at the case and obtained a reprieve.

Then there was the case of a teenager named Cordier, who got involved with two other young men in the killing of a sailor after a foiled robbery attempt. Here the jury saw only one thing, Cordier's prior offenses. "No sooner were we in the jury room than a tall, thin, white-haired 'foreman' pulled from his pocket a paper on which he had written all the charges against Cordier and, most important, his previous convictions. In truth these would dominate and determine this latest verdict. That's how difficult it is for a juror to not consider a previous conviction as an indictment and to judge a defendant outside the shadows that a previous conviction cast on him," Gide wrote.

Gide took his job as juror very seriously. In some cases he took notes during trials; at other times he took it upon himself to visit the families of convicted felons. In the Redureau case, a teenage servant, Marcel Redureau, hacked to death the family of his employer. It seems Marcel was set off by the father calling him a "lazybones" and telling the boy that he hadn't been at all happy with the boy's work for some time. "At this remark," Gide wrote, "the irked Redureau stepped down from the winepress, armed himself with a wooden hammer, a kind of fifty-centimeter-long bludgeon that was within his reach, and struck several blows at the head of his master, who sank down groaning, letting go of the bar. Then, seeing that he was still alive,

Redureau grabbed a huge chopper that the country folk call a grape bullock, which is used not on vines but rather to separate bunches of grapes that are pulled in the winepress. ...Redureau opened the throat of his master, who was in his final agony and soon gave his last gasp." Redureau then butchered the three children, the grandmother, the mother, and the housemaid.

Commented Gide:

"In no way do I presume to lessen the atrocity of Redureau's crime, but when a case is this serious, we have the right to expect that even the prosecution will be resolved to present for justice's sake all appurtenances, even those that might be favorable to the defendant — above all when he is an impoverished child, with no help other than a public defender."

Further testimony revealed that Redureau may have been affected by fumes from the wine press, but this theory was discounted when it was learned that the youth had worked primarily in the open air. Gide, finally, quoted the pathologist on the case: "Specialists who work on pubescent psychology have noticed that in schools the largest number of cases of subjects liable for punishment for bad behavior, disputes, and assault and battery occur in the fifteenth year, because on reaching that age, young people have minimal control of their primary impulses."

Gide recorded in his journals that a number of his friends dropped him after *Corydon* appeared. He also felt his public image succumbing to tabloid oversimplification. "The legend is gaining credit little by little," he confided in his journal. "The public knows nothing of me but the caricature. ...Even if some people have the curiosity to read me, they do so with such a mass of prejudices that the real meaning of my writings eludes them. They will end up by seeing in them what they have been told is there, and not see anything else." But more than fifty years after his death, Gide's reputation as a writer continues to rise, while taboos against discussing sexual matters, including non-normative sex, have collapsed, revealing just how far ahead of his time Andre Gide really was.

CHRISTOPHER MARLOWE

Christopher Marlowe (1564-1593) was born in Canterbury, England, into an impoverished family. His father was a shoemaker, his sisters all servants and washerwomen.

As a young student, Marlowe won a scholarship to Corpus Christi College, Cambridge. About this time, he became an actor and a secret agent in the service of Elizabeth I. After he received his MA in 1587, the London Theatre enjoyed a phenomenal success with his first play, Part I of *Tambulaine the Great*, the story of a visionary poet. The work became extraordinarily popular, and established Marlowe's reputation as a playwright. It was the first time a great poet had used modern English speech on stage.

The strong melody of Marlowe's blank verse helped create the saying, "Marlowe's mighty line." (Shakespeare later absorbed the style of Marlowe's cadences, infusing it with broad modifications.)

Some discrepancy exists regarding the chronology of Marlowe's works after *Tambulaine*, though most literary historians agree that *Dido, Queen of Carthage*, followed *Tambulaine* and then *The Jew of Malta* (1589), an abusrdist comedy that criticizes the posturing of Christian authority. In most of Marlowe's plays, his best lines are reserved for villain/heroes who defy the social, political and religious morality of their day.

Marlowe's personal life was somewhat notorious. Always outspoken, his freethinking opinions led to accusations of atheism, blasphemy, subversion and homosexuality. He once said, "All they that loved not tobacco and boys were fools." His belief that the Apostle John and Jesus had been lovers was freely aired at the time, and by the time of Marlow's death, he was being investigated for his blasphemous opinions.

Edward II—which details the defeat and murder of a gay king by corrupt barons—is considered to be his most accomplished play. The younger William Shakespeare learned much from Marlowe and generally acknowledged the older master's superiority until Marlowe's death in 1593. After this time, Shakespeare was able to develop on his own. "Shakespeare," as one critic wrote, "was only a couple of months junior to Marlowe, but he was later in starting and had a harder struggle, for quite young, he burdened himself with wife and family; an encumbrance Marlowe would never incur."

Marlowe's last play, *Doctor Faustus,* was the first dramatization of the Faust legend. Goethe was enthusiastic about the work and thought of translating it, once remarking, "How greatly it is planned."

It's thought that Marlowe's difficulties arose from his own temperament. He was brilliant, unstable and neurotic, though much loved by his many friends. Havelock Ellis writes: "It seems likely that the last years of Marlowe's life grew careless and irregular; his later plays show signs of swift and overhasty workmanship."

On June 1, 1593, in plague-ridden London, Marlowe got into a brawl with a man named Francis Archer in a tavern in Deptford, England.

Thom Nickels

"There was turbulent blood there," Ellis writes, "and wine; there were courtesans and daggers. Here, Marlowe was slain, killed by a serving-man, a rival in a quarrel of bought kisses."

The playwright had fought over a boy, perhaps a boy much like the one he describes in his poem, "Hero and Leander":

"I could tell ye
How smooth his breast was,
And how white his belly;
And whose immortal fingers
Did imprint
That heavenly path with
Many a curious dint
That runs along his back."

JOE ORTON

He was a semi-literate teenager who came from a poor family of six. He was asthmatic, spoke with a lisp and couldn't spell or put a simple sentence together. He'd also been fired from every job he had before he was twenty. "I wish I belonged to one of the idle rich and didn't have to work," he wrote in his diary. "I hate getting up to go to work in the morning."

Life is hard when you're destined to become one of the major playwrights of the 20th century.

Joe Orton educated himself by reading and listening to classical music. To correct his lisp and thick Leicester accent, he enrolled in a speech school. The problem not only was corrected, but Orton held the judges spellbound when he recited lines of dialogue from *Peter Pan* during a speech contest.

When still very young, Orton met classics scholar and aspiring writer, Kenneth Halliwell. Halliwell, older by seven years, was described by Orton's biographer, John Lahr, as "grave, pretentious and abrasive in his egotism." Halliwell and Orton took a small apartment where they dedicated their lives to reading and writing—an indulgence made possible by Halliwell's family inheritance. They'd spend their mornings writing and afternoons reading. When the funds were gone, they took jobs for six months so they could work at home the remainder of the year.

Halliwell, who had written several unpublished plays and novels, gave Orton the classical education he so desired, "assigning" authors such as Voltaire, Lucian and Aristophanes for young Joe to read.

The couple created their own personal "theater" in the defacing of books in the Islington library. Seems they'd steal art prints or cut out lewd photos and paste them inside books of etiquette, create false blurbs, or alter author's bios. After the damage, Orton would then love to hide in the library and watch the shocked patrons' reactions.

"The thing that put me in a rage," Orton said, "was when the Islington library told me they didn't have Gibbon's *Decline and Fall of the Roman Empire*, yet they carried so many rubbishy novels and books."

The two were charged with "malicious damage" to 83 books, removing 1,653 bookplates, and imprisoned for six months. Prison life changed Orton profoundly. "The old whore society lifted up her skirts," he wrote, "and the stench was pretty foul...it was the revelation of what lies under the surface of our industrialized society."

After his release, the BBC accepted Orton's short play, *The Ruffian on the Stair*. He then began his first full-length play, *Entertaining Mr. Sloan*. When the play opened in 1964, Orton was hailed as having "an exciting and unusual voice." One major theater critic said that the play, with its language and careful construction, was the best he had seen in 30 years. Many others, however, attacked Orton for his "disgusting physical perversions." Other plays like *Loot*, *The Good and Faithful Servant*, and *The Erpingham Camp* soon followed. In 1967, the Beatles engaged him to write a film, *Up Against It – a* project that Orton disliked and eventually came to naught. He wrote his farcical masterpiece, *What the Butler Saw* in 1967.

Oppressed by Orton's growing fame and his own literary failures, Halliwell's brooding intensified. Even sunny trips to Morocco, where they could freely indulge in hashish and boys, did little to alleviate his torment. On the night of August 9th, 1967, as Orton lay sleeping, Halliwell bludgeoned the playwright to death with a hammer and then killed himself with an overdose of sleeping pills.

Lahr wrote: "Orton expected to die young, but he built his plays to last."

D.H. LAWRENCE

He was a mama's boy who came from a working class background. Extreme physical delicacy plagued him from childhood. "I was born with bronchitis," he used to quip. Taunted and called girlish by his classmates, at home the young D.H. Lawrence suffered his parents' constant quarrelling. His possessive mother suffocated him; some say she did this to soothe the hurt of a rotten marriage. In his second novel, *Sons and Lovers*, Lawrence portrayed his coal miner father in a highly negative light. In later years, he decided that his profile had been much too harsh. From boyhood, he looked every bit the artist: his pale complexion and reddish blond hair framed eyes that looked wise beyond their years.

Lawrence was born on September 11, 1885 on Victoria Street in Eastwood, England. As a kid he fell hard for a local farm boy who helped him and his family at haymaking. He wrote about this relationship in his first novel, *The White Peacock*. In *Sons and Lovers*, he used the farm boy's sister as the model for the cold and detached heroine who remained unaffected by his (protagonist's) love, whereas the opposite was true: Lawrence was the cold and unresponsive one.

Average readers would not think of Lawrence as homosexual, but perceptive critics have noted that in all of his descriptions of sex with women, the sex is described from the receiving end. Lawrence typifies the sort of gay man who buries his true desires and allows himself to be swept away by strong and dominant women. Conventional marriages weren't uncommon for gay men in 1911, the year of his "capture by a voracious German frau, Frieda," according to one writer, who also added that, "Frieda had a way of making him feel like a man." In his novel, *Women in Love*, Lawrence used his good friend, Middleton Murray, as the model for Gerald Crich. In real life, the dark-haired, blue-eyed Murray was a handsome Apollo with whom some say Lawrence was in love. The wrestling scene in which Crich and Lawrence's alter ego "devour" each other in man-to-man combat depicts the two as coming together in a kind of boy ballet that stops just short of lovemaking. The implications are obvious. In those days, anything more than a wrestling scene would have spelled disaster for a literary career. The ending of *Women in Love* adds yet another jolt: when Gerald dies, his friend is so upset that his wife accuses him of brooding excessively about the death. "What are you worried about—you still have me! That should be enough!" she exclaims. He says it is not. It's here the novel ends.

Lawrence wrote twenty books, including novels, plays, essays and poetry. Some critics say that *Lady Chatterly's Lover* is not only autobiographical, but also a wish fulfillment fantasy for Lawrence, since there is anal sex between the gamekeeper and the woman. With Frieda, Lawrence moved to his favorite part of the world, Taos, New Mexico, where he befriended a young man named William Henry, a boy that Frieda disliked and would not allow on their property. In Europe,

Lawrence briefly associated himself with Lytton Strachey and John Maynard Keynes, gay men he disliked, not because of their overt homosexuality, but because of their "supercilious rationalism and boring talk." Plagued by asthma, bronchitis and bouts of influenza all his life, Lawrence once said that he was "a wretched object like a drowned ghost creeping downstairs to tea." He once said of Frieda. "She is a devil. I have been bullied by her long enough. I really could leave her now, without a pang." He also wanted to give up writing and become a gardener. "My gardens are so lovely, everything growing in rows and so fast," he wrote. Because of the sexual themes of his books, he was constantly under suspicion and his living quarters were often searched by the police. Before his death he wrote: "I am in the hands of the unknown God/He is breaking me down to his own oblivion/to send me forth on a new morning, a new man."

MARIANNE MOORE

Poet Marianne Moore, a friend of Ezra Pound, William Carlos Williams, and T.S. Eliot, liked to do chin-ups.

Visit the Marianne Moore Room at the Rosenbach Museum in Philadelphia, and you'll see the metal chin-up bar in the poet's reconstructed Greenwich Village living room. You'll also spot a 19th-century settee and bureau, a footstool (a gift from T.S. Eliot) and a painting of a yellow rose by e.e. cummings.

Personal belongings aside, the details of Moore's life remain as obscure as some of the meanings of her rhyming syllabic verse, verse the Cambridge Guide to Literature calls "marked by an unconventional but disciplined use of metrics, and a witty, often ironic tone." Nowhere in Dell Richards' *Lesbian Lists*, for instance — where Moore is listed as a famous lesbian poet — the *Cambridge Guide*, or Helen Vendler's 528-page critique of American poets, *Voices and Visions*, is anything stated about Moore's romantic life. What we do know is that she was born in 1887 near Kirkwood, Missouri, and that she lived with her maternal grandfather, the Rev. John C. Warner and her brother, John Warner Moore, who became an ordained minister in 1914. The family then moved to Carlisle and in 1916 to Chatham, New Jersey.

After graduating from Bryn Mawr, a publisher told the young poet she should forget poetry and become a secretary. Moore followed the publisher's advice for four years, though, in 1914, one of her works was published by Harriet Monroe's *Poetry* magazine. Other poems were published in *Others* magazine. According to Vendler, these early poems echoed Moore's concern that each work be part of a continuing effort to think through what poetry is. Though Moore would always examine painting, sculpture and decorative arts in her work—what Pound called "the logic of juxtaposition"—Vendler said Moore's way of writing became a search for identity. Moore herself called most poetry "prose with a heightened consciousness."

During most of her career, Moore condemned free verse, saying "it was the easiest thing in the world to create, with one intonation in the image of the other."

In 1918, she moved with her mother to a basement apartment in St. Luke's Place in Greenwich Village. The move was beneficial, since Moore believed that living in the city offered an "accessibility to experiences." New York also radically expanded her ideas about poetry. What once had been a search for personal identity—she followed Emerson's dictum that "artistic imitation is suicide," and avoided conscious references to other poets or poems—was transformed into a fascination for the world of trade and commerce. Because of commerce, Moore came to respect the values and inevitability of "influences." T.S. Eliot's collection of essays, *Sacred Wood*, also helped her see the value in the "existing monuments" of the past. Vendler writes: "It did not matter to Eliot's conception of tradition that individual works—the *Odyssey*, *The Inferno*, or *Paradise Lost*—might have been written hundreds or even thousands of years apart; what mattered was that all those works existed simultaneously in the mind of the person sitting down to write a poem."

Her first book of poems was published in 1921, her second, *Observations*, in 1924. In 1921, she began to write free verse, and in 1926, she became editor of the prestigious literary magazine, *The Dial*. Her *Collected Poems* (1951) received the National Book Award and the Pulitzer Prize.

Before her death in 1972, Moore willed her literary and personal papers, as well as the contents of her living room, to the Rosenbach.

DAVID NORRIS

David Norris' election to the Irish Parliament in 1985 made him the first openly gay person to be elected to any nation's parliament. But the politician, James Joyce scholar and foreign affairs expert prefers to downplay this because he does not wish to be known as "a freak" or a "professional fairy."

"Today I talk about gay rights if it emerges as part of a context that means that people will listen with interest.... If I were going off all the time monotonously and incessantly, they'd get browned off and bored," said Norris in 1997 when he visited Philadelphia to perform a one-person monologue on the works of James Joyce.

Norris is the person most responsible for getting Ireland's sodomy laws off the books. The Offense Against the Person Act of 1861 called for life imprisonment for anyone convicted of sodomy. It was a revision of Henry VIII's 1536 punishment of death by hanging, and the notorious La Bouchere Amendment, which criminalized "acts of gross indecency between males."

Norris' role began in 1974, when he heard his colleagues say there was no discrimination in Ireland.

"I'm discriminated against as a gay person," he announced, mindful of the arrests of men in parks and public lavatories—the only available meeting places for gay men at that time. Norris organized a group that counseled those arrested on sodomy charges, and the group appealed a number of cases. Encouraged by legal victories, his group worked to remove anti-gay laws that penalized everything from sodomy to prolonged handshakes or looks among members of the same sex.

When Norris decried La Bouchere as a "nasty piece of legislation," Norris' challenge exposed him to banter cruel enough "to peel the paint off the ceiling." It was that law under which Oscar Wilde was convicted of sodomy; but it would also claim two Royal Air Force soldiers for trading "lascivious looks" in the mid-50s, Norris said.

In 1976, the Irish gay rights movement became the Campaign for Homosexual Law Reform.

"One way to challenge the law was the constitutional route," he said. "But anyone who was found with their pants down in the bush—the last thing they want is publicity. They just want to disappear."

Norris offered himself as a test case, a difficult maneuver since he had never been arrested. Instead he used his life as a gay man with the potential to be arrested for looking or having sex with a man. The case went to the high court in 1974, where Norris' barrister was Ireland's future president, Mary Robinson.

"I made sure that, in addition to the legal points, we had a showcase trial, because I wanted to blow away the cover of secrecy surrounding homosexuality," he said.

The press had a field day.

"They covered the trial on the front page with these internationally reputable authorities placing their views on record," he said.

The judge, although impressed by the statistical evidence and the high number of homosexuals in Ireland, ruled to maintain the law because of the Christian and democratic nature of the Irish Constitution, Norris recalled.

The case was appealed to the Irish Supreme Court, which voted 3-2 against Norris in 1986. This was overturned in 1988 by the European Court on Human Rights, an inter-governmental court that may challenge any European country's Supreme Court ruling if it threatens the rights of minorities or human rights groups.

Afterward, in 1993, there was a movement to pass an age-of-consent law that gave an older age for gays. Norris and his group asked Minister of Justice Marie Geoghegan-Quinn to speak with Phil Moore, a prominent politician whose son is openly gay.

Norris believes that meeting turned the tide.

"She absolutely refused to consider the discriminatory legislation regarding the age of consent," he said.

HART CRANE

Harold Hart Crane is one of the major American poets of the twentieth century. Largely self-educated (he never went to college), his body of work is astonishingly small for a poet who some rank next to Whitman and whose work has influenced giants like Robert Lowell and Dylan Thomas.

Crane was also queer, and in John Unterecker's remarkable biography, *Voyager*, the poet's struggle for artistic and sexual independence in the dark era of 1932 can be seen as a role model for young queers struggling with similar situations today.

For instance, he was only seventeen when he left his home in Akron, Ohio, for New York City. He knew no one in New York but that didn't interfere with his determination to mold himself into a poet and find himself as a man. He began by submitting poems to *The Pagan* and to Margaret Anderson's *The Little Review*, and he established a network of influential friends like Sherwood Anderson, Max Bodenheim and Malcolm Cowley. Poetry, however, didn't pay the bills. Often financially destitute, he'd return to Ohio with his tail between his legs.

Once he'd licked his wounds, however, Crane would be back in Manhattan for another go-round.

He came out in a letter to a friend when he confessed the sex of the person he was in love with ("This 'affair' has been the most intense and satisfactory one of my whole life, and I am all broken up at the thought of leaving him. Yes, the last word will jolt you," Crane wrote). The affair didn't last, though Crane was to have many others, including a long relationship with Emil Opfer, a merchant marine. But love for Crane was often short-lived and filled with disillusionment. His letters, for instance, are filled with tales of sailors and rough trade he picked up along Manhattan's waterfront. He even writes of a chimney sweep he brought home who tracked charcoal across his living room rug.

Crane was sometimes the target of thugs and homophobes during his midnight prowls. Though his growing alcoholism did nothing to hone his powers of discernment, his eventual undoing on the afternoon of April 27, 1932 was as much society's fault as his. Conflicted feelings about his homosexuality — a psychological by-product of The Dark Era — seemed to place him into a permanent "I'm the only homosexual in the world" mindset, a case scenario that people coming out in today's far more permissive zeitgeist, often with help from organizations and support groups, experience as a temporary roadblock. With Crane, however this self-loathing seemed to be an indelible stamp on his consciousness.

Take his candy manufacturer father ("Crane's Candies"), who spent a lifetime berating him for wasting his time on poetry and not becoming a successful businessman. Crane's agonizing stints through every profession imaginable — ad salesman, journalist insurance agent — never panned out and his life, from the moment he left Ohio, was an epic struggle accommodating the artistic demands of his nature with the practical demands of the world. After the publication of *The Bridge (to Brooklyn Bridge)* and his earlier collection, *White Buildings,* he was able to amass grants and enough money to travel to Paris and Mexico, but even this was not enough to save him.

"Whitman's 'immediate experience' embraced an America simple enough for his daily life to absorb it. Crane inherited a jungle of machines and disintegrating values which he had no discipline to manage and which soon destroyed him," his friend Waldo Frank wrote in 1947.

On April 27, on his way back to Manhattan from Mexico, Crane had some trouble with some sailors on the ship, *Orizaba.* Refusing his offer of companionship, they reacted like a (homophobic) tangle of machinery and beat him up. This was the last straw. The poet walked to the stern of the ship, took off his coat and quietly leaped into the sea.

DJUNA BARNES

Born June 12, 1892, writer Djuna Barnes spent much of her childhood under the tutelage of her grandmother, Zadel Barnes.

At 16, Barnes married 52-year-old Percy Walker; the marriage lasted two months. Djuna then enrolled in the Pratt Institute in Brooklyn but left after six months.

In New York, she met German-born Ernst Hanfstaengle. They became engaged during World War I but separated when Hanfstaengle said he couldn't tolerate Barnes' interest in women and announced he wanted a German wife.

In 1913, Barnes began writing for 'The Brooklyn Daily Eagle.' Calling journalism "rubbish," she became successful with her celebrity interviews and series of "stunt" articles such as "How It Feels to be Forcibly Fed" and "My Adventures Being Rescued" for *The Sunday World.*

Though she considered herself an artist first and a journalist second, Barnes often went to great lengths to get a story (for the rescue piece, she trained with novice firemen). Phillip Herring, author of *Djuna*, writes: "But that which she valued little sold well; that into which she poured her soul was often seen by editors to be a less valuable commodity."

Her 1915 poetry collection, *A Book of Repulsive Women*, was something she came to loathe.

When McCall's magazine sent Barnes to Paris in 1921 to interview James Joyce, she met Thelma Wood, the love of her life. She and Wood took an apartment on the boulevard Saint-Germain and were often seen walking along the Left Bank in their matching black capes and hats.

Plagued by lifelong money problems, Barnes was forced to sell the copy of the proof sheets of *Ulysses* – a gift from Joyce – for $125. Benefactors like Natalie Barney (whose Paris mansion was the center of lesbian culture at the time) and Peggy Guggenheim saved Barnes from extreme poverty.

The Ladies Almanack, a satire on Natalie Barney's lesbian circle, was published in 1928. The following year, Barnes and Wood separated.

Barnes left for New York in 1930, where she began writing plays in the style of John Millington Synge. She became involved with Margaret Anderson's 'Little Review' and had an affair with Anderson's lover, Jane Heap, which ended her tie with the magazine. Her masterpiece, *Nightwood*, was edited by T.S. Eliot and published by Faber & Faber in 1936.

"I find myself having to struggle, directly after reading, not to ape myself; and very few writers exercise this pull," Eliot wrote of Barnes' work, which has been compared to Herman Melville, Emily Bronte, Joyce and Ernest Hemingway.

Barnes died in 1982 at the age of 90. Called the "Garbo of Literature" because she loved solitude, Barnes once told a young Susan Sontag (who had sent her a copy of *Against Interpretation* but who was afraid to speak to her on the street): "You have refrained from addressing me, because someone has told you that I am a demon.... Please do me the pleasure of speaking with me the next time?"

SUSAN SONTAG

I first heard Susan Sontag lecture in 1967 when I was a teenage journalism student. Gay but in the closet at the time, I'd heard that Sontag had written an essay on Camp that included many homosexual references. This was encouraging to me since there were few intellectual references to homosexuals in public forums in those days. Feeling that Sontag was a possible bookish ally, I convinced my best friend at school to accompany me to the Free Library to hear her speak.

Sontag's *Against Interpretation* had just been published (*Styles of Radical Will* would be published shortly thereafter), and her name was being bantered about because of the Camp essay. The Vietnam War, then in full swing, was also beginning to season her political and antiwar views. She was, as they say, "hot property."

Dubbed "The Dark Lady of American Letters" because of her good looks and her reputation as a brainy wunderkind—"The Natalie Wood of the U.S. Avant-garde," as *Contemporary Biography* declared—many saw her as the successor of novelist/essayist Mary McCarthy. 'Dark Lady' or not, at the Free Library podium in 1967 she certainly presented a memorable persona. Walking onstage in an opera cape, she had a habit of whisking her great mane of hair off her forehead while taking periodic tokes from a long black cigarette holder. These personal touches or images suggested Oscar Wilde and the opulent poetry of Baudelaire.

That night at the Free Library, a double exposure of sorts occurred when her son, David Rieff, who seemed his mother in miniature with his dark clothing and long dark locks, escorted her to the podium.

"What a pair!" I remarked to my friend then. "Do you believe it?"

Unfortunately, I was so entranced by Sontag's hair tossing and smoking I forget what she talked about, but I left wanting to know more and resolved right then and there to read everything she wrote.

When I moved to Boston after journalism school I met a Harvard professor, Jon, who told me that he once befriended Sontag in the most unlikely place: Provincetown, where he owned a house. After meeting Susan at the seaside resort, he wound up giving her a lift back to Boston in his convertible MG. Picturing Sontag's massive head of hair blowing in the wind, I asked him to tell me what they talked about, what happened, for by that time, Sontag was even more famous. Her anti-Vietnam War tome, *Trip to Hanoi*, had just been released and she was the talk of Cambridge and Harvard.

I was eager to hear whatever gossip Jon could offer about his encounter, however inconsequential or tabloid-like, but when he called her a "pushy dyke," I was shocked. "How can she be a lesbian and not be open about it?" I wanted to know. Those were the days of gay liberation, when truth and honesty were worth their weight in gold, when the closet was just as objectionable as napalm and Richard Nixon. By way of retracting his statement, Jon did manage to tell one story: On the drive back to Boston, Susan spotted a handsome hitchhiker and urged Jon to give him a lift. Back in Boston, Jon said, Susan and the hitchhiker disappeared into the sunset together—or more accurately, a hotel.

Sontag, it is said, was livid when the book, *Susan Sontag, The Making of an Icon*, by Carl Rollyson and Lisa Paddock, published by W.W. Norton and Company, surfaced in 2000. Reading the book, I duly noted that it corroborated several of Jon's early allegations regarding her sexuality. So...*is* she or *isn't* she? She is a lesbian, the book's authors contend, but refuses to come out—a fact that irked many gay activists for a while, among them Kate Millet [*Sexual Politics*] and ex-*Village Voice* dance columnist Jill Johnston, who wrote an early lesbian manifesto, "Lesbian Nation." Johnston understood why Sontag remained in the closet, and she was gracious in her comments. "Everyone in the family 'knows,' but no one is supposed to mention it (except in the context of a rumor mill), much less go abroad with it," she wrote.

As the authors of *Susan Sontag: The Making of an Icon*, wrote: "A few years after the appearance of *Notes on Camp*, Sontag suspected that Jill Johnston was about to publish an article about her sexuality. Sontag phoned Johnston, hurling all manner of insults and managing to convey her horror that Johnston might out her. Sontag had become agitated, Johnston remembers, because Roger Straus (her publisher) had warned her of the dire consequences of such an article."

Sontag's "hiding" irked me for a time until I decided that it didn't matter what she did in the privacy of her bedroom. Sontag's philosophy and her opinions have always championed pro-gay and pro-freedom causes anyway, so what did it matter? In the 70s she made occasional appearances at New York Gay Academic Union and granted interviews to national gay magazines. Having come to believe that Sontag was "special," I just had to accept that. And if she kept mum on the subject of her sexuality, well, who's to say there might not be an object lesson in that?

After the Free Library lecture I encountered Sontag again at a theatre symposiums at Penn, after which I didn't see her for many years. In the interim I tried to read everything she wrote, with the exception of her fiction, although I did read her early novels, *The Benefactor*, and *Death Kit*. While I had a soft spot for her short stories, I relished her essays more than anything else.

When she came to Temple University in the 1980s to conduct a graduate seminar in writing, I tried but failed to secure an interview with her. Appreciative of my efforts, she telephoned me and later wrote a note explaining that her time in Philadelphia "had been 'compressed.'" Her courtesy seemed to open the door for a possible interview at a later date.

The next time I saw her was at the Free Library in the 1990s (where she had come to discuss her theatre work in Sarajevo). At that occasion my chat with her included a mention of my long-lost friend Jon and the ride he'd given her in his sports car so many years before.

"My God, that was a long time ago," she said, looking at me as if I'd just dislodged a personal cobweb. I drew back, afraid that I had offended her somehow. Some years passed and then she popped up at a Rosenbach Museum function where she spoke on photography and the poetry of Marianne Moore. Once again we had an opportunity to chat, albeit on the run, as she was headed out to dinner with the Rosenbach brass.

"Philadelphia is so weird," she said, laughing. "What other American city would put a clothespin in the middle of downtown?"

Another Sontag visit—the most recent—this time at the Kelly's Writer's House at Penn, drew a mellow and serious crowd of people over a two-day span. Sontag came as part of the Kelly Writers House Fellows 2-day Program, where she read from her work and participated in a Q and A following an informal (and delicious) breakfast. Moderator for the Q and A was Penn professor and Kelly Writers House Faculty Director, Al Filreis.

I arrived late for breakfast (nobody on campus seemed to know where the Kelly Writer's House was located), but once there I joined the crowd hovering around a lavish table filled with fresh fruit, bagels, coffee, pastry, cream cheese and orange juice. At one point I bumped somebody's elbow in my quest for cream cheese; alas it was Sontag herself, opting for the same cream cheese platter.

The intimate Kelly Writer's House gathering topped any Sontag event I've ever attended.

During the Q and A I asked Sontag how she weathered the storm caused by her essay on Sept. 11 in *The New Yorker*.

The essay was written in fifteen minutes, she said, and she didn't think it controversial at all when she sent it off. In the piece she asked what, in American foreign policy, may have contributed to the tragedy. After the essay's publication, the vehemence with which she was attacked—she was called a traitor among other things—was unlike anything she'd experienced to date, she said. Even her anti-Vietnam war stance did not attract the same kind of hatred and viciousness, which even including death threats.

In essence Sontag said that the new attitude of intolerance is indicative of the change that has taken place in America, that G. W. Bush and his neocon crowd have more or less implemented a kind of silent takeover, that the Republic we once knew is rapidly becoming a full-blown Empire. "The Republic is over, America as we knew it is over," she said, at the same time cautioning that even when we throw "these scoundrels out" — meaning the Bush administration — American foreign policy will never be the same.

Saying she was in Berlin when 9/11 occurred, she added that had she been in Manhattan that day she would have had a clear view of the burning towers from her apartment building rooftop. "I thought about what I would have felt...that maybe I would have tried to get downtown to help, along with friends of mine, to work with the people finding bodies. I am sure I would have been drawn to help them," she said.

Sontag, who described herself as antiwar as opposed to a pacifist ("In a small number of circumstances there is a justification for war"), questioned whether visual images alone can turn one against war. "I've come to think that the only way one can be persuaded to change is by narration; it's never an image alone," she said. "One can change one's mind by reading a book or viewing a film but never by simply [viewing] a photograph.

"In Paris I saw the coverage of the war on Iraq. I saw on the front page of a French newspaper a photo of a huge, burly US soldier with Darth Vader-like gloves pinning a small Iraqi man to his knees. The context of this, in a French paper, is American power — 290 million people — vs. Iraq's 24 million people, half of whom are under 19. Yet I saw a similar image in the United States but the context here says that it's an American soldier subduing a looter and restoring order. So, images do not speak for themselves."

She cited the unholy alliance between religion and politics in America, something that was noticed by de Tocqueville in the 1800s as something peculiarly American. In America today you cannot get anywhere in politics without claiming Jesus Christ as your personal savior; gone are the days when a president like FDR could stay home from church on Sunday. Sontag was quick to point out that American politics and nationalism have corrupted religion, that American Christianity has been bastardized in order to sanctify a right-wing political agenda.

"We live in a culture where selfishness is highly valued. It's called individualism," she said. "You are thought to be a chomp, a dope, if you put other people's interests ahead of your own. Only patriotism is the least attractive way of not being egocentric."

In her essay on Paul Goodman many years ago, Sontag said how she relished going to Paris, a place where (keeping in mind that reading, for Sontag, was everything) she could live for a year without reading books.

"Reading is a promoter of inwardness. It encourages us to have an inner life. It strengthens the possibilities of having an inner life. You might say we all have an inner life but it gets pretty thin if you don't nourish it." Without nourishment, she added, the inner life can turn to worrying about our jobs, what's for dinner, what someone said to us, holes in our socks or God forbid, Jennifer Lopez's latest film role. "That's pretty much what your inner life devolves into if you're not nourishing it," she said.

Sontag admitted being an accumulator, mentioning the thousands of books in her personal library.

"Sometimes I stand in front of the shelves and dream about what's in them. I remember what's in them. The books in my library are like a map of the world, so it is very important to me how they are arranged."

To write, however, one must at a certain point let the books go and begin the work. Her book, *Regarding the Pain of Others*, is really one long essay, she said. "When I write essays I am much more at sea than when I write novels. When I write novels or stories I really do have the story before I start, or at least I think I know. With essays it's all harder and nebulous in the beginning. I know that an essay is something that concerns me or obsesses me all the time and then I think about writing the essay and finding out what I think. Usually there's a lot more rewriting than there is with fiction."

Who were her favorite essayists? Walter Benjamin, Paul Valery, Roland Barthes and Ralph Waldo Emerson. " I spend as long as a year on an essay, on something that's only 25-30 pages long. Most people do not want to put that much time into an essay. Maybe I'm crazy to have done it myself."

Sontag thought this is a great period for the essay and that people today are more interested in essays than they are in fiction.

"*The New Yorker*, for instance, in the old days used to publish two stories every issue. Now they publish one story and some issues have no story at all. *The New York Times Book Review* will put non-fiction first and fiction second in the table of contents."

She confessed that she often had the feeling she wasn't writing the books she really ought to have written but rather devoted her time to writing projects that demand her attention. "I have this idea that when I just get past this point, then I can start the work that I really want to do—maybe I'll turn into a completely different writer two or three years from now if I get all this forty-year spell of juvenilia out of my life...."

Somehow I don't think 'juvenilia' is the right word.

Sontag's death at age 71 of leukemia at 7:10 AM on December 28, 2004 surprised everyone, although the news barely made the rounds on broadcast television.

Whereas *Today's* Katie Couric prattled on endlessly about the accomplishments of Jerry Orbach, an actor whose death-date was shared with Sontag's, Sontag herself wasn't even given a cursory nod. Only the print media—a full page essay and obit in *The New York Times*—and the BBC seemed to recognize the importance of this woman who many believe was one of the most original and brilliant thinkers of the past 100 years.

The truth is that writers, especially writers who speak truth to power, aren't valued much in the "dumbing-downed," Divided States of America.

The New Yorker pined, "Susan Sontag, who wrote for this magazine on and off for more than thirty years, died last Tuesday, to everyone's surprise, for though she had been in treatment for cancer intermittently since the nineteen-seventies, she never got it into her head—or, therefore, into anyone else's—that this disease might kill her."

Around the world, reactions to her death differed. Those who hated her, such as the bloggers on *Free Republic.com*, a conservative website, had a field day: "Priestess of The Cult of Anti-America," one writer labeled her. "Susan Sontag's death at 71 was at least four decades overdue," another contributor wrote. "...An enthusiastic promoter of homosxuality, an admirer of Sartre, an outspoken advocate of the Muslim side in the Bosnian war and in Kosovo," another offered. "The gap between Ms. Sontag's heart and mind was total, reflecting the soul of a rootless purveyor of self-hate...." And: "The leading advocate of 'human rights' was not only a hypocrite and a fraud to boot, she was also a moral degenerate terminally devoid of human compassion and common decency." Such is the viciousness of right-wing intolerance in the "D"SA.

A more reasoned op-ed piece in 'The Los Angeles Times' by Patrick Moore, examined Sontag's life in the closet.

"In a 2000 *New Yorker* profile, Sontag outed herself as bisexual, familiar code for 'gay,' yet she remained quasi-closeted, speaking to interviewers in detail about her ex-husband without mentioning her long liaisons with some of America's most fascinating female artists.

"She may well have felt that her true sexuality would limit her impact in the male-dominated intellectual elite, while an omnisexual charisma opened doors...."

Regardless of the topic, Sontag's writing was always provocative, and always sparked her readers' curiosity — not a surprising ability, considering that David Rieff once referred to his mother as "the most curious person alive."

As writer Doug Ireland in *The LA Weekly* concluded, "Susan is not replaceable. She will be missed."

✦

GEORGE SANTAYANA

Americans philosopher George Santayana was born in Madrid in 1863 and emigrated to the United States with his family in 1871. After the move, he dropped the original form of his name, Jorge Ruiz de Santayana y Borrais.

The family settled in Boston, where the young philosopher was educated at Harvard, later becoming a professor of philosophy at the university from 1889 to 1912.

In 1912, after concluding that life in the United States was not for him, Santayana returned to Europe. By this time he had already published his five-volume *The Life of Reason*, a study of reason in science, art, literature, and everyday life. In this masterwork, Santayana concludes that the only reality is matter itself and that all else arises from man's experience of, and response to, matter. He took this idea further in his book, *The Realm of Being*, a four-volume study that included the book, *Skepticism and Animal Faith*.

In Europe, he met Frank Russell, the elder brother of philosopher Bertrand Russell. Frank Russell was dashing, masculine and smart but also hopelessly heterosexual. Santayana's first meeting with Russell was climactic in the extreme. He was on an outing with

Bertrand Russell and some friends when they met. Since he happened to be walking a plank while boarding a boat, this first glimpse of the mesmerizing elder Russell caused him to lose his balance and almost fall into the water.

While the force of such an attraction never drove Santayana over the edge, the relationship's unconsummated 40-plus-year history did prevent him from having another major love interest. When Frank Russell was imprisoned for bigamy in the 1880s—"the result," historian A.L. Rowse wrote, "of Russell's excessive heterosexuality"—Santayana consoled Russell with these words: "It seems almost as if I had gathered the fruits of your courage and independence, while you have suffered the punishment which the world imposes always on those who refuse to conform to its ways."

Despite the philosopher's devotion, he did not blind himself to the Russell brothers' faults. About Bertrand Russell, he wrote: "There is a strange mixture in him of great ability and great disability; prodigious capacity and brilliance here—astonishing unconsciousness and want of perception there." Some claim that is what made Bertrand Russell so brilliant at mathematical logic and such a fool at human affairs.

Santayana once wrote to Frank Russell, "You now say more than you ever said to me, even in our young days, about being 'attached'...to me; you must have been in some way which...I don't pretend to understand." Santayana admitted that although Frank Russell played a major role in his life, he was only a bit player in Frank's—a sad commentary, especially considering that Frank could never even remember Santayana's name and often called him, "Sergeant."

Santayana wrote one novel, *The Last Puritan*, in 1935. By all accounts the novel was a disaster, despite its heartfelt profile of Frank Russell. He also published three studies dealing with American life. His memoirs, *Personas and Place,* was published in three volumes. He also wrote *Egotism and German Philosophy,* a study of German nationalism that preceded World War II.

"Santayana," wrote Rowse, "is the most philosophic spirit of the 20th century—in the wildest and most useful sense of the word."

Santayana had a critical intelligence that never lost touch with the intuitional. "This made him," as Rowse has noted, "probably the best writer of English prose in our time."

✦

French Philosopher
MICHEL FOUCAULT

Hailed as the most influential French philosopher since World War II, by the time of his death from HIV/AIDS in 1984 at age 57, Michel Foucault's views on prison reform, psychiatry, modern medicine, queer politics and pedophilia had made him a controversial figure.

As a youth, Foucault was a mediocre student who was transferred from one school to the next. He studied philosophy at Ecole Normale Superieure and later taught psychology to philosophy students in the town of Lille. His first book, *Histoire de la Folie*, was actually his thesis. The manuscript was rejected by Gallimard (a noble tradition in France: Gallimard's Andre Gide rejected Proust's first work). The work was eventually published by M. George Canguilhem, who admitted being dazzled by the book's study of the relations between madness and unreason during the classical epoch. Roland Barthes described the book as "audacious." Other critics, especially Jean-Paul Sartre, called the book "muddled and confused." Generally, the book was greeted with indifference and silence.

"Throughout *Histoire de la Folie*," wrote David Macey, author of *The Lives of Michel Foucault*, "Foucault hints at the existence of a muffled noise that resists confinement's attempts to silence it. The voice is heard in the works of poets like Gerard de Nerval and Antonian Artaud, in the last paintings of van Gogh, in the madness of Nietzsche."

Foucault was to write many literary reviews and articles. He defined Flaubert as the first Modern, the literary equivalent to Manet ("The one who paints with constant reference to the museum."). His second book, *Les Mots Et Les Choses*, was published in 1965 and became a bestseller. The book explored such varied subjects as philology, economics and natural history.

Susan Sontag first introduced Foucault's name to the American public in her book *Against Interpretation*. Foucault's study of the French prison system, *Suicides de Prison*, was published in 1973. Called "the professor militant," Foucault participated in many demonstrations and acts of civil disobedience on behalf of French workers, the war in Vietnam, the rights of immigrants, and solidarity with Palestine. He also supported the rights of terminally ill people to commit suicide, and he believed that age of consent laws for children should be lowered to 13 or 14. "Children," Foucault wrote, "can and do seduce adults."

In 1973, he attended meetings of the Front Homosexual d'Action Revolutionnaire, though he feared gay ghettoization and believed that 'gay' could be as oppressive a label as any other. He thought that the writing of gay novels by gay people was not a very beneficial activity and that the notion of 'gay painting' bordered on the absurd. He denounced the identification of homosexuality with "love between young men," saying: "This corresponds to a reassuring canon of beauty.... It destroys the disturbing element in affection, tenderness, fidelity, comradeship, for which a fairly controlled society cannot make room."

In his personal life, he enjoyed drugs such as marijuana and LSD, and frequented New York's Mineshaft. His companion of many years was Daniel Defert, though Foucault was often spotted leaving his apartment late at night dressed in leather. He shaved his head every morning so it would look less obvious that he was losing his hair. He wore a white turtleneck because he detested ironing shirt collars. He also loved the sensual life he discovered in California. He had a near-death experience after being struck by a car. "For maybe two seconds," he wrote, "I had the impression that I was dying and it was really a very, very intense pleasure. The weather was wonderful. The sun was descending. It was, it still is now, one of my best memories."

✦
HERVI GUIBERT

From author David B. Feinberg's bitter memoir, *Queer and Loathing,* to the writings of Paul Monette or Larry Kramer, AIDS writing is fast leaving its mark on world literature.

French writer Hervi Guibert (1955-1991) wrote extensively on AIDS. After his HIV diagnosis, he vowed to turn himself "into a human fountain pen," and wrote even during bouts of amnesia or when lacking sufficient motor control. Guibert viewed his affliction, unlike Feinberg, with a kind of flippancy, joking in his 1989 novel, *L'Incognito,* that he contracted HIV from reading the newspaper. In his 1990 book, *To the Friend Who Did Not Save My Life,* he wrote that AIDS "was a disease that gave death time to live and its victims time to die, time to discover time, and in the end to discover life, so in a way those green monkeys of Africa had provided us with a brilliant modern invention."

Throughout his life, but especially when he was sick, Guibert preferred writing and the company of books to people.

Edmund White, writing in *The Burning Library,* states that when Guibert was 28, he had "an earnest, wide-eyed, almost somnambulistic manner, devoid of the irony and bitchiness characteristic of his extremely rude generation in Paris." The blond, blue-eyed writer/photographer/film-maker was also philosopher Michel Foucault's best friend. The friendship between the two men culminated in Guibert's portrayal of Foucault as Muzil in *To the Friend*.

Guibert thought of himself as following in the footsteps of Rimbaud, de Sade, Nietzsche and Thomas Bernhard. When he was a photographer and critic for *Le Monde*, he specialized in sadomasochistic photography. His first photography volume, *Les Chiens*, had images of masters treating slaves like dogs by forcing them to walk on all fours while consuming chunks of meat. His second collection, a series of portraits of friends, including Gina Lollobrigida and Foucault, had a Hallmark-card sweetness despite the fact that Foucault is pictured in a dressing gown.

Guibert's first novel, *Voyage Avec Deux Enfants* (1982) was followed by *Les Lubies d' Arther* (1983) about two gay sadists who travel the world terrorizing people. His third book, *Des Aveugles*, was published in 1985, and later became a play.

"Guibert had never felt squeamish about rubbing his reader's nose in all his bodily excretions," White wrote, referring to the Guibert's American counterpart, Dennis Cooper. White described the delight Guibert took in shocking polite society with novels about torturing teenage boys or writing about skateboarding youths with ugly faces and beautiful bodies—for example, *Fou de Vincent* (1989), the story of a skateboarding kid who kills himself while stoned. In *Mes Parents*, an autobiographical work, the narrator's mother scolds her gay son when she discovers love letters from another boy. The son hisses, "When I'll lean over your dead bodies, my dear parents, instead of kissing your skin, I'll punish it, I'll pull out a hank of your hair."

Guibert committed suicide on December 27, 1991, after living with AIDS for one year.

Great Music was the Backdrop for the Love of
BENJAMIN BRITTEN and PETER PEARS

One of the 20th century's most notable musical collaborations had its genesis in a gay marriage that lasted for nearly 40 years.

Composer/pianist Benjamin Britten was born in Suffolk, England, in 1913, three years after tenor Peter Pears' birth in Surrey. The two men met in 1936. By that time Britten had established himself as a brilliant musician at the Greshman School and the Royal College of Music in London, and Pears was singing with the BBC Singers.

Britten's father wanted him to become a farmer; his mother saw him as a great musician. The die was cast when an organist at St. Paul's Cathedral suggested that the boy's talent be allowed "to grow undisturbed into flame," after which time Britten began to make a name for himself on the London concert stage.

Peter Pears' nonmusical lineage consisted of clergymen and military officers. At the time of his enrollment in the Royal College of Music in 1933, he didn't know whether he was a baritone or a tenor. His insecurity paralleled Britten's on another plane: a sense of personal emptiness that Britten's friend and artistic mentor, W.H. Auden, summed up when he wrote: "To my friend, Benjamin Britten, composer, I beg that fortune send him soon a passionate affair."

The prayer to fortune worked. Soon Britten was writing in his diary: "Peter Pears is a dear and a very sympathetic person, though I'll admit I am not too keen on traveling on his motorbike." The meeting was a catalyst for Pears' as yet unfocused talents: The two musicians soon collaborated on a BBC-commissioned program about Michaelmas Day. Britten sketched the music to an Emily Bronte poem; Pears was the tenor. "He is a good singer and a first-rate musician," Britten wrote. Pears, meanwhile, thought that Britten had an "extraordinary connection between his brain and his heart and the tips of his fingers."

Britten wrote that his early relationship with Pears was a "friendship based on the intellect." It was in Toronto, while the two worked on Britten's *Variations on a Theme of Frank Bridge* — a joint recital — that love blossomed. Homosexual relations between consenting adults were illegal in Great Britain at that time, so both musicians pretended to have separate bedrooms when they were photographed for a popular magazine. Incidences of people scrawling the word 'pansy' over posters announcing Britten-Pears recitals were not uncommon.

During WWII, both men became conscientious objectors. "The whole of my life has been devoted to acts of creation, being by profession a composer, and I cannot take part in acts of destruction," Britten told the conscientious objector tribunal. Britten incorporated his pacifist feelings into his antiwar Requiem Mass, *Sinfonia de Requiem,* at his 1941 Carnegie Hall debut. His 1944 opera, *Peter Grimes,* which he wrote for Pears, alienated London critics with its treatment of homosexuality and conscientious objection.

Of all Britten's works, *The Seven Sonnets of Michelangelo* comes closest to being a testament to his union with Pears. Pianist Graham Johnson commented that the piece was "a garland of songs to celebrate a marriage of minds and heart." Graham's statement should not be interpreted to mean that the two men did not diverge on occasion. For career reasons there were temporary separations as well as sideline flirtations. Still, Leonard Bernstein observed that for Britten, Pears represented "all relationships put together, which made it difficult for him to have other deep friendships."

While music helped maintain this intimacy, the couple's sexuality was not discussed honestly until after Britten's death. Critics then began to see Britten's homosexuality as an important factor in the composition of such works as *Billy Budd,* an opera on the ethos of manly affection, and *Death in Venice,* a controversial work that incorporated Pears' idea on the role of Apollo.

Britten died in 1976 in Peter Pears' arms; Pears followed him 10 years later.

"Love is blind," Pears wrote to Britten in 1971, "and what your dear eyes do not see is that it is you who have given me everything, right from the beginning—I am here as your mouthpiece and I live in your music."

ADRIENNE RICH

Amilestone in the metamorphosis of poet Adrienne Rich—from a married mother of three to radical lesbian feminist—occurred in 1963, when she began to explore feminism in her work.

By this time, she had already established her reputation as a poet with her first book, *A Change of World*, a collection of poems praised by W.H. Auden as proof that whatever Rich wrote "shall, at least, not be shoddily made."

Born in 1929 in Baltimore, Rich was educated at Radcliffe College. After graduation, she was awarded a Guggenheim Fellowship, and spent a year traveling in Europe. In 1953, against her parents' wishes, Rich announced her engagement to Alfred H. Conrad, an Eastern European Orthodox Jew. Her family did not attend the wedding, claiming their daughter's match to be with "the wrong kind of Jew."

The union produced three sons. Shortly after Rich ended the marriage, Conrad committed suicide.

After her divorce, Rich moved to New York, and became involved in Vietnam War protests and the civil-rights movement. Her poetry began to be influenced by filmmaker Jean Luc Goddard's use of language and images. Her feminist vision also grew with her reading of James Baldwin and Simone de Beauvoir. In de Beauvoir especially, she found much to admire, despite de Beauvoir's marginalization of lesbian issues.

In *Split at the Root,* Rich wrote: "In New York, the suppressed lesbian I had been carrying in me since adolescence began to stretch her limbs, and my first full-fledged act was to fall in love with a Jewish woman."

At this time, she also was having dreams while asleep of arguing about feminist politics with her lover.

"I had been, more or less, a Jewish heterosexual woman," she wrote. "But what did it mean to be a Jewish lesbian? What did it mean to feel myself, as I did, both anti-Semite and Jew?"

In 1974, she shared the National Book Award with Allen Ginsberg. In 1981, the National Gay and Lesbian Task Force gave her its Fund for Human Dignity Award.

In her essay, "Compulsory Heterosexuality and Lesbian Experiences," Rich analyzes the characteristics of male power, citing the use of women in male trans-actions, the imposition of male sexuality on women, and the exploitation of female labor: including motherhood.

The so-called "shared common cause with male homosexuals," she wrote, is hampered by the "quail-tative differences in female and male relationships," citing anonymous sex and the "pronounced ageism in male homosexual standards of sexual attractiveness" to be two such stumbling blocks.

But it is in the workplace, she wrote, where women "have learned to accept male violation of their psychic and physical boundaries as the prices of survival. Women," she states, "have been educated by romantic literature and pornography to perceive themselves as sexual prey."

Adrienne Rich has lived with writer/editor Michelle Cliff since 1976.

FLORENCE NIGHTINGALE

Poet Adrienne Rich must have had Florence Nightingale in mind when she wrote, "The drive to self-knowledge, for women, is more than a search for identity; it is part of our refusal of the self-destructiveness of male-dominated society."

That same male-dominated society expected Florence to remain within the parameters of her wealthy socialite family. There she could be admired and attend parties, occasionally using the French and Greek her father taught her in an era when a classical education was reserved for men. "Frivolous and a waste of time" was how Florence described her life as a social butterfly. By that time, she says she had already heard the voice of God directing her to perform some service for humankind. Though the pursuit of this quest led her to consider converting to Catholicism and becoming a nun, her transcendent spirituality soon negated the attractions of organized religion. Years later, as a hospital administrator during the Crimean War, she'd comment on the nurse-nuns under her charge: "They flitted about like useless angels worrying about souls while leaving the bodies dirty and unmanageable."

Considered more attractive than her sister, Parthe, Florence was expected to marry a prosperous gentleman. Her family also reminded her that she should forget this "mission from God" nonsense and just delight in the social whirl. It would take Florence more than a decade to decide what her special mission in life was to be.

She had two long-term engagements to men her family expected her to marry. Her relationship with Henry Nicholson lasted seven years. It is assumed that Florence tolerated this relationship only because she was in love with Henry's sister, Marianne. "I have never loved but one person with passion in my life and that was Marianne," Florence wrote. One way to keep Marianne in her life was to stay with Henry, a not-uncommon arrangement amongst many 19th century lesbians. When Henry insisted on setting a marriage date, Florence ended the relationship, an action that not only angered her family but made Marianne so furious she stopped being Florence's friend.

Another suitor, Richard Milnes, an editor, was engaged to Florence for six years. Florence likewise ended *that* engagement when Mr. Milnes insisted on a marriage date. Her female mentor during this time was her father's sister, Aunt Mai, a woman as intellectual and spiritual as she, a woman, Florence said, who was like a lover to her.

Nursing in 1847 was not considered an honorable profession because it was seen as attracting prostitutes and drunkards. Hospitals knew nothing of sanitation procedures; many let human excrement pile up on the floors. Cleanliness utilized as a means of preventing disease was Florence's idea. Still, when Florence mentioned nursing as her life's mission, her horrified family opposed her plans for ten years. Undaunted, Florence studied medical journals at home and waited for the right time to act.

In 1853, with her family's support, she was hired as a superintendent of a hospital for women. She reversed the facility's unsanitary condition, which meant clean blankets and bedding, clean clothes, and decent food. Within a short time, because of her insistence that wounded Crimean War soldiers and other patients be treated like human beings, she came to be regarded as a living legend. She championed the use of anesthesia for operations, was one of a few nurses who didn't desert her post during a major cholera outbreak, and did much to help bring sewage treatment and clean water to India.

In 1907 Florence Nightingale was the first woman to be awarded the British Order of Merit. This secular lesbian saint died peacefully in her sleep three years later.

HAROLD ACTION

Born in 1904, writer Sir Harold Action was many things: poet, art collector, Commander of the Order of the British Empire, tutor to the English royal family.

As a member of one of the wealthiest families in Europe, he achieved notoriety when novelist and ex-lover Evelyn Waugh portrayed him as the comic and decadent Anthony Blanche in *Brideshead Revisited*.

In Action's case, great wealth and privilege hampered his ability to live openly as a gay man. The one exception was his sojourn to Beijing, where he worked as a member of the British Intelligence Service and was able, because of his social status, to attract the attention of young Asian men. This was just one of the many benefits of a large allowance and future inheritance Action struggled to maintain. To do this, he had to endure further humiliation from his father, Sir John, who thought nothing of locking the family villa whenever his son stayed out late with young men, thereby forcing Action to scale the mansion walls like a delinquent intruder.

James Lord wrote in "Some Remarkable Men" that "Harold happened not to be handsome, and for a homosexual, that unfortunate fact usually makes for a lifetime of emotional inferiority.... The brilliant intellectual can never believe himself to be on terms of equality with the handsome, thoughtless lords of the playing fields."

But Action learned to use extravagance in behavior and attire to compensate for his looks. He wore gray bowler hats, and had massive side-whiskers; his intelligent conversational style attracted the likes of T.S. Eliot, Lytton Strachey, D.H. Lawrence and W. Somerset Maugham.

Because beauty could never be his, Action lavished attention on material objects, including his art collection, a private library of 50,000 volumes, and six private villas, including La Pietra, the chief family estate in Florence. He transformed these villas into "lordly pleasure houses," or...beautiful extensions of his unattractive physiognomy.

At age 58, this prisoner of privilege remained without the things he most craved: a mutual love interest and the freedom to live openly as a gay man. Even his father's death did not free him from the conflicts of the closet. In 1986, he threatened legal action when he objected to a reference of him as a homosexual in a biography by writer Nancy Mitford. Asked by friends why he would dispute the truth, Action said, "I don't deny it. My position is delicate now that I am close to the royal family. What would Princess Diana think if she should read such a thing about me?"

Despite a lifelong opium habit, Action published several books, including two volumes of memoirs, novels and a study of Gian Gastone de Medici.

"I had made mistakes and wasted my talents, but I looked upon my failures as steppingstones toward the more beautiful and the most beautiful," he wrote in *Memoirs of an Aesthete*.

Those "steppingstones" included installing Alexander Zielcke, a handsome straight man, into La Pietra. It was a relationship that had all the elements of a commercial acquisition—a relationship that James Lord describes as marked by a coldness because of Action's fear of "spiritual responsibility and need for self-effacement that enduring love inevitably entails."

Action died in 1994.

MICHELANGELO
became Obsessed With the Male Nude.

Michelangelo Buonarroti was born the son of a wealthy governor in Caprese, Italy, 1475. With a decline in its fortunes, the family was forced to move to Florence, where the future artist was sent to live with a stonecutter.

There, Michelangelo became interested in stone and spent his days at the local quarry. When his mother died, he returned to live with his father and uncle, a tense situation because both men regularly beat Michelangelo to "drive the artist out of him."

In 15th-century Italy, manual labor was considered demeaning, and artists were considered no better than artisans. Thus, throughout his life, Michelangelo bore the scars of his father's disapproval.

"I was never a painter or sculptor like those who kept shops," the artist wrote in 1548. "I always kept the honor of my father and brother, and although I have served three popes, it was through force."

A career break of sorts occurred when Lorenzo de Medici took Michelangelo into his household, at which time the young artist began to support his family with work commissioned by Medici.

Until his death, Michelangelo reminded his family that his labors were for them, although he believed that his family neither respected nor appreciated what he did for them.

By the time he began working for Pope Julius II, Michelangelo already had established his reputation as a violent and terrible man. Because these character traits were applied to the pope as well, the two were in constant conflict, with Michelangelo storming out of projects, later returning to ask the Pope's forgiveness.

"The fierce and bearded old warrior, Julius, who had commissioned it, was the prototype for the Sistine God," wrote Margaret Walters in her essay on Michelangelo in *The Male Nude*. A powerful erotic feeling runs through a great deal of Michelangelo's religious art; the spiritual can hardly be separated from the sensual."

Walters adds that the artist was obsessed with the male nude, and that he had no understanding of the female body, which "he considered inferior and even a little frightening."

"Most 19th century critics denied Michelangelo any sexuality at all," Walters wrote. "Even today, it is a common ploy to argue that his genius inhabits some transcendently bisexual—and therefore, nonsexual—realm."

Michelangelo's sexuality was intense, though he attempted to hide his homosexuality for fear of scandal.

He wrote love letters to one of his models, Febo di Poggio, and he courted 15-year old Cecchino dei Bracci, about whose beauty he wrote: "With his face God wished to correct nature." When dei Bracci died in 1544, at the age of 16, Michelangelo designed the boy's tomb and wrote at least 50 poems mourning his death. The love of his life, however, was the young Roman aristocrat Tommaso de'Cavalieri, whom he met when

Michelangelo was almost 60. de'Cavalieri, who was married and had three children, would remain Michelangelo's close friend until the artist's death in 1564

Michelangelo, ashamed of his ugliness and broken nose, completed his masterwork, *David*, when he was 29. The 18-foot-high statue stands as his idealized self-image. The artist would later distort his view of The Body and utilize it as a channel for his spiritual aspirations.

His most stunning male sculpture, *Victory*, illustrates this distortion. A handsome young male stands over an old man he has defeated in battle. Despite the youth's beauty, he has the beginnings of a sagging belly, something Walters insists is "the monstrous embryo of the old man who is the young god's future shape."

Michelaneglo died in 1564 at age 89.

HENRY JAMES

Writer Henry James was born in 1843 in New York City and educated by private tutors until he was 12. When he was a teenager, his family moved to Europe, where he attended schools in France, Switzerland and Germany.

Returning to the United States, he entered Harvard Law School, but left after one year to concentrate on his writing. This hiatus resulted in his being published in *The Atlantic Monthly* and *The North American Review*.

By 1869, he had completed a farce, *Pyramus and Thishe*, and in 1878 he published his first novel, *Watch and Ward*.

In 1872, he traveled to Europe, where he befriended Turgenev, Flaubert and Zola. He eventually settled in London, where his circle of friends expanded to include Joseph Conrad, Stephen Crane, H.G. Wells and Ford Madox Ford, writers who later would dub him "The Master."

The stuffy, patrician side of James' personality blinded him to the talents of men like Oscar Wilde, whom he dismissed as "a fatuous fool" and "a tenth-rate cad." James' critical intelligence, always an excellent asset in writing, tended to impede his growth in other areas, however — namely sexuality: It wasn't until he was in his mid-50s that he realized he was gay. This truth became self-evident when he met a handsome, blond sculptor named Hendrik Andersen, 30 years his junior.

Andersen used the writer as a catalyst for his own career, accepting favors only if they served to benefit him professionally.

James, already wary of associating with the intellectuals, saw in Andersen the earthy simplicity he looked for in sailors and workmen. As a result, he tolerated the sculptor's antics.

A.L. Rowse wrote in *Homosexuals in History*, that Andersen was always making huge sculptures that James wanted him to scale down, and that once he made a bust of James "as unexpressive and wooden as the sculptor was unresponsive."

Before returning to the United States in 1890, James published *Roderick Hudson, The American, The Europeans,* and *The Portrait of a Lady.* His best works include *The Ambassadors* and *The Golden Bowl.*

In 1890 he turned to drama and wrote drawing-room comedies. He also wrote a number of travel books and received honorary degrees from Harvard and Oxford.

He also became romantically involved with socialite Jocelyn Persse (during which time Hendrick Anderson continued to pursue the writer) and Harvard graduate Morton Fullerton.

In 1915, James became a British citizen. That same year, he suffered two strokes, but lived to receive the Order of Merit from King George V. Henry James died on February 28, 1916.

Baseball's
GLENN BURKE

Glenn Burke, who "invented" the high-five, was called the next Willie Mays after signing with the Los Angeles Dodgers in 1976. In 1982 the handsome, 6-foot, 210-pound African American centerfielder became the first Major League baseball player to come out of the closet.

Nicknamed "King Kong" and "Speed Demon" by his teammates, Burke played Major League baseball for four seasons, including the 1977 World Series, before homophobia forced him to retire.

Born in 1952, Burke realized he was gay at the height of his popularity as a Dodger centerfielder. His determination to lead a double life led him to tone down an impressive .300 batting average so that he wouldn't be in the limelight.

"Becoming a star and a hot commodity, my secret would be leaked out," he wrote in his 1996 memoir, *Out at Home*.

Burke also admitted a fear of being blackmailed and followed by teammates when he ventured to the gay clubs in San Francisco.

"In the '70s, the Dodgers were drawing 3 million fans a year," Burke wrote in *Out at Home*. "They had a pristine, clean image. Management was afraid of my sexual orientation, even though I never flaunted it. To this day, the Dodgers deny trading me because I was gay.... Baseball was not ready to acknowledge gay people."

Burke also writes in *Out at Home* that the strain of living a lie peaked after the 1977 National League Championship series with the Philadelphia Phillies.

Burke became so depressed that he began using marijuana and cocaine regularly. His relationship with the gay son of Dodger manager Tommy Lasorda, Spunky, who occasionally cross-dressed, was also taking its toll. When word leaked out about his life, there was panic of sorts among some teammates.

A few wore towels whenever Burke was in the locker room, while others warned their friends not to bend over in the shower. The Dodgers paid Spunky to end his association with Burke, and the Dodgers' general manager, Al Campanis, promised Burke a bonus if he would marry a woman.

Burke's refusal to marry was based on his zero tolerance for what he called in his memoirs, "America's emphasis on living the straight and narrow lifestyle." This emphasis, he wrote, "forced famous gay athletes to marry women they didn't love just to save face."

"The Dodgers knew I was gay, and were worried about how the average father would feel about taking his son to a baseball game to see some fag shagging fly balls in centerfield," Burke wrote. "But the fact is, baseball has the same percentage of homosexuals as there is in mainstream society...but baseball, more than any other sport, promotes masochism and virility."

Burke's refusal to conform got him released from his Dodgers' contract. He went to spring training with the Oakland Athletics in 1979. The Athletics was a team that was past its prime, and from which he would soon retire after being the target of a homophobic slur from manager Billy Martin.

Burke, in *Out at Home*, quotes Martin as having told teammates that he "wasn't going to have a faggot on any of his teams."

After retiring, Burke found some solace playing for various San Francisco gay softball leagues.

Sadly, Glenn Burke died in 1995 of HIV-AIDS.

HILDA DOOLITTLE
Built the Imagist Movement

Early photographs of poet Hilda Doolittle show an elegant young woman who, in many ways, resembled actress Glenda Jackson in Ken Russell's 1969 film, *Women in Love.*

Born in 1886 in Bethlehem, Pennsylvania, to a father who was a University of Pennsylvania astronomy professor, and a mother who was a pious Moravian, Doolittle at 15 was, according to poet William Carlos Williams, "…tall, blond, with a long jaw and gay blue eyes."

In 1895, the family moved to Upper Darby, Pennsylvania, where her mother's religious beliefs (in Moravian theology, all souls are female, and Christ is the husband of the male, as well as of the female), began to form the foundation of young Hilda's growing poetic consciousness and eventual attraction to ancient Greek culture.

In 1901, at a Halloween party on Penn campus, she met poet Ezra Pound, then a handsome, muscular undergraduate. Their relationship and eventual engagement flourished during Doolittle's two-year tenure at

Bryn Mawr College—until Pound abruptly ended the romance.

Doolittle later followed Pound first to New York, and then to London, where she agreed to meet him on the steps of the British Museum in order to show him samples of her poetry. Pound admired the brevity and the easy rhythm of Doolittle's verse, and helped launch her career as a poet.

In his amusing but cryptic essay on Doolittle in *Prophets and Professors*, Bruce Bawer asks how Pound could build a poetry reform with imagism around the works of a poet named Hilda Doolittle.

"So, before Pound tipped his hat and departed...that day, he scrawled something at the bottom of the manuscript of *Hermes:* 'H.D. Imagiste. Voila!' The pathetic, pretentious and much-patronized Hilda was Hilda no more."

But Pound abandoned H.D. again—this time as a poet and not a lover—when another poetic school (vorticism) caught his eye.

By this time, Doolittle, as H.D., was already published in Harriet Monroe's Poetry magazine and in *Des Imagistes*, the 1914 anthology of imagist poets.

Though intimate friendships between women were commonplace early in the 20th century, women with lesbian or bisexual inclinations were categorized as spinsters or pressured into heterosexual marriages.

As a result, many women's self-awareness of lesbian feelings usually occurred later in life. Doolittle's own "discovery" was not actualized until after her 1913 marriage to poet Richard Aldington, which lasted several years.

In the 1920s, Doolittle met writer/filmmaker Winifred Ellerman, who used the pseudonym, Bryher. One of the richest women in England, Bryher supported

Doolittle and provided her with a comfortable life so she could write.

According to Barbara Guest, author of *Herself Defined: The Poet H.D. and Her World*, their relationship was more of a business companionship. True perhaps, but Bryher's love and commitment to Doolittle was the driving force behind a union that lasted 40 years. Bryher published several of Doolittle's books, including her 1926 autobiographical novel, *Palimpsest*.

Though Doolittle's novels were panned by critics as "slack and self-indulgent," her work attracted the attention of T.S. Eliot and D.H. Lawrence. Her collected poems include: *Hymen* (1921), *Heliodoroa* (1924), and *Red Roses for Bronze* (1929).

Doolittle chose not to publish her explicitly lesbian works during her lifetime. *Pilate's Wife*, *Asphodel* and *Hermione* were published after her death in 1961.

His Homosexual Holiness,
QUENTIN CRISP

Author's note: this interview with Quentin Crisp occurred shortly before his death.

Quentin Crisp is sitting in one of the downstairs bars in Philadelphia's 2-4 club, drink in hand. He's had an exhausting day. He's just finished his one-man act—*An Evening With Quentin Crisp*—at the Wilma Theater, a moderately attended event that seems crowded compared to the poor turnout at the 2-4 gathering.

Crisp is on a sofa facing the tiger-stripped bar. Beside him is a member of the Wilma staff and beside her, a box of Crisp's books, ready for autographing. But nobody is buying, despite the fact that this ninety-year-old gentleman put on quite a show, commenting on everything from Princess Diana to Seattle's bounty of lesbians and Christmas trees. Crisp, in fact, is really a latter day Oscar Wilde (he can quote Marlene Dietrich and Saint Theresa in the same breath). At the show's end the audience gave him a standing ovation, but not before asking him questions about life and love, youth and maturity, his sex life: "Are you a top or bottom...?" — figuring they'd better ask while the legend's still around to answer.

Crisp became a prominent figure with the publication, in the 1970s, of his autobiography, *The Naked Civil Servant* — an account of his life in London, where he freely wore mascara and lipstick in the streets. Beaten up nearly every day because of his looks, Crisp learned to look unkindly on his native England. Today, for instance, he refers to England as "a savage country."

"In England I never felt safe," he told me earlier that day in the Doubletree hotel. "People were shouting at me from out of nowhere, throwing things at me. I suppose it was the way I looked. You see; the English do not like effeminacy. They do not like effeminate women. Englishmen are always saying of their girlfriends, 'Oh you know, she is always fiddling with her appearance and asking how she looks.' An Englishman calls his wife 'Old Girl.' Who wants to be called 'Old Girl?'

Crisp wrote books on lettering and window display before the publication of *The Naked Civil Servant* brought him international notoriety. Though movie options for the book failed, its transformation into a PBS teledrama brought it into countless living rooms, something Crisp says would not have happened, had it been made into a feature film. "Movies about homosexuals," he says, "are only seen by homosexuals and liberals who wish to be seen going into the theater...everybody else ignores them."

As Crisp's left hand is paralyzed, he can only type with his right. The paralysis occurred several years ago, in the same month that his literary agent dropped dead. Both were signs, Crisp believes, that his writing career had come to an end.

These days Crisp spends his days napping and doing nothing. He reads little, with the exception of the books he's coaxed into writing blurbs for ("For which I am not paid!" he emphasizes). He never reads to expand his mind, and can no longer write letters or send cards to people. What he *does* do is accept invitations to lunch (he is listed in the Manhattan telephone directory). He likes a place called the Bowery Bar because it's plush and Sylvia Miles used to perform there. Still, Crisp likes his food bland; he wants food to taste like "nothing."

I've seen Crisp in films and videos for years, but when I first saw him in person at the Doubletree I was struck by his tiny frame and demur manner. Old age, of course, had reduced his much larger film image into the visage of a frail sparrow. I immediately felt the need to protect him, to hold his hand — despite the serpentine harshness of some of his opinions.

At the 2-4 gathering he said he is received favorably wherever he goes, with the exception of San Francisco. "I think they thought I was someone touring the length and breadth of the land delivering a manifesto," he says, "but when I never mentioned homosexuality, their love for me died."

Crisp says he also lost the love of the homosexual community when he said that Princess Diana was trash and got what she deserved.

"I don't know how she became a saint," he says. "She was a Lady before she became Princess Diana, so she knew the racket. Royal marriages have nothing to do with love. You stand beside your spouse and you wave, and for that you never have a financial worry until the day you die and you are photographed whenever you go out — what more could she want?"

He talked about the lonely and miserable life of 'the homosexual' and mentioned how every gay person knows this to be inherently true, although everyone pretends it is not. And yes, if someday in the future a pregnant woman aborts her baby because he has the 'gay gene,' he would understand: "Who wants to be gay anyway?"

These aren't the kinds of opinions that are going to get you invited to an HRC dinner, or win election as Grand Marshall of the next LGBT march on Washington, so don't even talk about equal rights. The gay movement, Crisp says, is too shrill. "Anger begets anger. If you shake your fist in the face of society it will react. Why do gays want marriage?" he asks. "I used to think that the hatred of homosexual men was chiefly envy because of their freedom—because gay men were always making love to people they found exciting, whereas 'real men' were always making love to people they find thoroughly distasteful."

He says he's been celibate for almost fifty years. "Even when I was 40 I no longer had a love life. As soon as you can no longer be thought of as a boy, you've had it—after that you pay. As I've never loved anybody the way I love money, I'm never going to do that."

During the Q&A at the Wilma, Crisp was perfectly charming, and when he was escorted about the stage, looking like a watered down Victorian Ghandi, one felt a certain holy presence—not quite His Homo Holiness, but something else that many very old people seem to possess. I found that no matter what he says, you can't quite get mad at him because it's obvious that his soul really belongs to another era.

"Happiness is never 'out there,'" he insists. "It is within you. Never let your happiness reside in other people."

He believes this, even as he awaits death—"When you're old, you hunger for it," he told the Wilma audience. Never one to linger too long in any one mood or sentiment, he quickly rebounded by quoting Marlene Dietrich on love: "You have to let them put it in or they don't come back."

"Don't you just love that line," he says wistfully.

Ah, the old days.

Philadelphia's
THOMAS EAKINS

In 1886, he scandalized the burghers and upper classes of Philadelphia when he ripped the loincloth off a male model at the Pennsylvania Academy of the Fine Arts. As a result of this action, he was forced to resign his post as well as his membership at the Philadelphia Sketch Club. More scandals ensued, such as accusations of incest and bestiality made by his brother-in-law. A repeat of the loincloth incident at Drexel University saw the University canceling his lecture series. Finally, Eakins left provincial Philadelphia for the relative isolation of New Jersey, where he was embraced by another exile, poet Walt Whitman.

Eakins had been offending the Philadelphia bourgeoisie well before the loincloth incident. As writer Adam Gopnik wrote in an essay on Eakins in *The New Yorker*: "All Eakins' studies of the male nude have about them...a powerful charge of desire, and Philadelphia, sensing the presence of a code, even if they couldn't figure out the precise meaning of the message, acted oppressively. They knew that there was an Other in there somewhere, and they threw it out."

'The Other' was the homoerotic content of his art, though biographers say that Eakins did not lead any sort of overt gay life. Gopnik wrote, "A hidden homosexual life in 19th century Philadelphia would not leave much of a record behind; yet, especially in the case of someone as well known as Eakins, such a life would be unlikely to go completely unremarked."

As a teacher, Eakins often photographed himself and his students in the nude. One platinum-print portrait of himself and student J. Laurie Wallace, was a study for his homoerotic, *The Swimming Hole*. Critics noted how the stance of both Eakins and Wallace resemble the pose of both Donatello's and Verrochio's *David*. Copnik wrote that most of Eakin's photographs are of men, and are much more "posy," self-consciously sexual, than his photographs of women. "Many of these men are young and androgynous, and in some of the photographs the male nude has assumed an 'odalisque' pose—stretched out facedown on a rug, or reclining asleep on a draped couch—which in 19th century art was normally adopted only by women," Gopnik wrote.

Although he married Susan Hannah MacDowell, Eakins met a young Irish lad named Sam Murray, and their intense friendship lasted 30 years. Eakins and Sam took long trips together into remote parts of the wilderness. It's also interesting to note that Murray married a woman several months before Eakins died, and then, only after a 20-year engagement. Ultimately, whether the relationship between Eakins and Murray was ever consummated is beside the point: Eakins always valued the Greek aesthetic and his photographs of naked men in athletic endeavors like rowing, boxing, swimming, and wrestling formed the basis for his comment that "the male form is the most beautiful in nature."

Allen Ellenzweig in *The Homoerotic Photograph* wrote that Eakins' relationship with Murray was not unlike "the romantic friendships that the older Walt Whitman established throughout his life with several working-class men, particularly the omnibus driver, Peter Doyle. For both Eakins and Whitman, these sharp differences in age and intellectual capacity mirrored the requirements of ancient homosexual courtship where, as Foucault has it, 'truth and sex were linked, in the form of pedagogy, by the transmission of a precious knowedge from one body to another.'"

Born in Philadelphia in 1844, Eakins went to Central High School, where he learned technical drawing. In 1886, he went to Paris, catching French realism before it evolved into Impressionism. From Paris he wrote to his father: "The big artist does not sit down monkey-like and copy a coal scuttle or an ugly woman like some Dutch painters have done nor a dung pile, but he keeps a sharp eye on Nature and steals her tools."

In Paris he learned to have no shame about bodies or sex, a fact that would cause him trouble on his return to the Quaker City. 1870 found him in his parent's house on Mount Vernon Street, where he'd set up a portrait studio, doing pictures and portraits of society people and members of the Roman Catholic hierarchy. His sporting pictures include such masterpieces as *Max Schmitt in a Single Scull*, and *Pushing for the Rail*. "Like the best sports writing, they are at once detailed to the point of being overdone and relaxed to the point of being underplayed," one critic commented.

He exhibited at a Philadelphia gallery in 1896, an event that was ignored by the local press. When the Pennsylvania Academy awarded him the Temple Gold Medal for a portrait of an archbishop, Eakins accepted it wearing red bicycle pants, and then gave the medal to the U.S. mint, where it was melted down.

Eakins died on June 25, 1916. He was buried in a forgotten West Philadelphia plot that remained unmarked until 1983.

WALT WHITMAN

The tour guide at the Walt Whitman house in Camden was adamant: "Mr. Whitman was not a homosexual!" Glancing at a 1982 issue of *Parisian Review* magazine [containing the essay, "Whitman and the politics of Gay Liberation"] I asked her to put in Whitman's desk, she mentioned that Whitman's nurse, Mary Oakes Davis, had been in love with him. Then she quoted Whitman's infamous line to the gay John Addington Symonds when Symonds confronted the poet on the homoerotic content of the Calamus poems in *Leaves of Grass*.

"...I am fain to hope that the pages themselves are not to be even mentioned for such gratuitous and quite at the time undreamed and unwished possibility of morbid influences — which are disavowed by me and seem damnable."

Edward Carpenter, a contemporary of Symonds', knew that Whitman was lying. He blamed Whitman's cowardice on the social atmosphere of 1891. Carpenter claimed to have slept with Whitman and gave details of the encounter to a gay writer named Arthur Gavin. Then there were Whitman's male lovers: ex-Confederate soldier Peter Boyle [a thin Irishman who was the poet's companion for 15 years]; Warren Fritzenger [the male nurse who took Whitman along the Camden waterfront in his wheelchair]; William Sydnor [a lad who drove a Pittsburgh streetcar]; David Fender — "a redhaired young man," Whitman wrote; John Ferguson, "tall and slender," and Willy Hayes, "a drummer boy in a marine band." There was also 14-year-old Walter Dean, whom Whitman met in Wanamaker's [John Wanamaker, the so-called "King of Merchants," banned *Leaves of Grass* from Wanamaker's bookstore]. "A fine boy," the poet said of Dean in one of his Day Books.

I left the small, Mickel Street house not having convinced the housekeeper that Whitman was gay, even though thousands of other visitors — academicians, poets, critics, writers — had all heard the same talk from this [otherwise gracious] lady who went out of her way to insist that what the old bard did in his favorite swimming hole, Timber Creek, was just take mud baths with the local boys. No doubt she'd also insist that WW's stint as a Nurse in Washington, DC during the Civil War had nothing to do with the availability of male soldiers to love and care for.

Whitman's childhood was a lonely one. His father, like poet Hart Crane's, was convinced his son would be a failure and wanted to drive the poetry nonsense out of his head. For a while Whitman took a job as a schoolteacher and became editor of a newspaper in Brooklyn. Those early years saw the poet as quite the dandy, since he had a special fondness for expensive clothes. In his book, *Specimen Days*, he wrote of his explorations of Long Island and the New Jersey beaches [especially Cape May], of his walks around Manhattan and Philadelphia. He often went to the opera at the Academy of Music. His best spot for meeting boys was near 4th and Market Streets.

One of his constant companions was the 15-year old Bill Duckett. Whitman met the boy when he was 65 years old. On May 1, 1886, Duckett moved in with him, invited, no less, by housekeeper Mary Oakes David, a woman who specialized in marrying old men so she could gain their inheritances. The apex of the Duckett-Whitman relationship occurred when Duckett escorted Whitman onstage at New York's Madison Square Theatre.

Leaves of Grass brought scores of visitors to the poet's Camden abode. Oscar Wilde was among those who came. In 1888, Whitman suffered a stroke that left him bedridden until his death. When he died, the neighborhood boys raided the huge stock of champagne he kept in his basement.

As Whitman once told the sculptor, Sidney Morse, "...I detest lemonade...if one is going to drink anything—champagne, abstemiously taken, goes to the spot and don't make a fool of a fellow..."

CHARLES STODDARD

After the publication of *Leaves of Grass*, Walt Whitman attracted the attention of a 24-year-old writer named Charles Stoddard. Just as other young men were attracted to Whitman (16-year old Bill Duckett, teenagers Will Wallace and Harry Stafford to name a few), Stoddard took it upon himself to write the poet and send him samples of his work.

Born in 1861, Stoddard grew up in San Francisco and worked in a bookstore there when his first poem was published in a magazine edited by Samuel Clemens and Bret Harte. In 1864, he traveled to the Hawaiian Islands, the origin of the first letter to Whitman. Stoddard waited in vain for a reply, then sent another. "I ask," he wrote, "why will you not speak to me?"

In his second letter, Stoddard talked about Hawaii. "For the first time I act as my nature prompts me. I would not answer in America, as a general principle, not even in California, where men are tolerably bold." He told Whitman about the native boy he'd fallen for: "I go to his grass house, eat with him his simple food, sleep with him upon his mats, and at night sometimes waken to find him watching me with earnest, patient looks, his arm over my breast and around me.... Do write me a few lines for they will be of immense value to me."

"I do not write many letters, but like to meet people," Whitman replied. "Those tender and primitive personal relations away off there in the Pacific islands, as described by you, touched me deeply. In answer to your request, I send you my picture—it was taken three months since."

In 1899, Stoddard published his "A South Sea Idyll" in San Francisco. The tale detailed his affair with a 16-year-old native boy named Kana-ana, whom Stoddard said "would mesmerize me into a most refreshing sleep with a prolonged and pleasing manipulation." Taking his romantic happiness for granted, Stoddard convinced himself he needed a change and made preparations to return to civilization. Leaving the island on a boat, he watched his distraught lover swim after him, an agonizing scene he'd remember for the rest of his life. Even as Stoddard watched Kana-ana chase the boat, he vacillated, hoping for a shipwreck or that somehow the boy would jump on board. Kana-ana, of course, did not make the boat but disappeared on the horizon.

Experiencing another change of mind, Stoddard soon wrote Whitman that he must "get in amongst the people who are not afraid of instincts and who scorn hypocrisy," and said that he was "numbed with the frigid manner of the Christians; barbarism has given me the fullest joy of my life."

By the time he retuned to live in Hawaii several years later, Kana-ana was long gone. Later, he left the islands to become Professor of English at Notre Dame University and later a lecturer in English literature at Catholic University of America.

Though Stoddard and Whitman never met, Whitman said of him, "He is of a simple direct naïve nature, never seemed to fit in very well with things here: many of the finest spirits don't—seem to be born for another planet—seem to have got here by mistake..."

Before his death in Monterey, California, Stoddard was secretary to Mark Twain, and lived for a while in Italy, England and Cambridge, Massachusetts.

The reason for Stoddard's resignation from Catholic University was his earlier fascination for youths like Kana-ana. Despite his earlier to conversion to Catholicism, his primary allegiance seemed pointed towards the principles of another sacred scripture, Whitman's Calamus poems.

EDWARD CARPENTER
Friend of Walt Whitman

Known as a "Victorian gentleman in revolt," Edward Carpenter's philosophy of gay male love established the groundwork for an international gay movement that influenced the work of sex researcher, Havelock Ellis, novelist D.H. Lawrence and John Addington Symonds. Lawrence was especially interested in the male bonding possibilities of what Carpenter called "homogenic love," though later in life he and his wife Frieda would come to deny homosexual implications in Lawrence's novels.

Born in Brighton, England in 1844, Carpenter, in his autobiography *My Days and Dreams*, described himself as an "oversensitive, clinging child raised in a household of sisters." In 1870, he was ordained an Anglican priest, passing up an opportunity to tutor Queen Victoria's grandchildren, and for a while was curate of St. Edward's in Cambridge.

His life changed when he read Walt Whitman's *Leaves of Grass*. Whitman's spiritual egalitarianism was a factor in his decision to leave the priesthood. He also wrote free verse in the style of his mentor, publishing *Towards Democracy* in 1883. He studied Hinduism, theosophy, reincarnation and vegetarianism, and created a minor scandal by wearing sandals into the British Museum to do his research.

Carpenter's books include, *Love's Coming of Age*, *The Art of Creation*, and *The Intermediate Sex*, in which he used the term Uranian (from Uranus, or heaven) to mean homosexual. "This new human type will probably become in affairs of the heart, to a large extent, the teachers of a future society, thanks to their immense capacity of emotional love," he wrote.

Carpenter advocated "triune" (heterosexual) marriages (but not sexual promiscuity) in which couples are not completely exclusive, but broaden their base of romantic operations to include the occasional "other."

Attracted to various socialist movements of the time, he was more interested in society's reform and a return to rural crafts than in political revolution.

A high point of his life was his trip to America to sit at Walt Whitman's feet. This extraordinary mentorship landed him in Whitman's bed, despite the vast difference in their ages. Carpenter, in fact, would later come to recommend Whitman's method of sleeping next to a young man in order to recharge an old body. The method included massage, stroking, kissing, but not necessarily orgasm.

When Symonds asked Whitman whether the word "adhesiveness" in the Calamus poem meant sexual relations between men, Whitman lashed out at such "morbid influences — which are disavowed by me and seem damnable."

Carpenter, however, knew otherwise. He knew that Whitman was running scared. After all, this was about the time of the Oscar Wilde trials.

In old age, Carpenter demonstrated to a young 20-year old (writer Arthur Gavin) how Whitman made love. The method began with the laying on of hands. "He was in no sense a succubus like so many old men, draining the young man of all the vitality they can get, like a vampire. The emphasis was on the caressing and loving.... There are so many possible relationships and one misses so much if one limits oneself to one sex or color or age," Gavin wrote.

Edward Carpenter died in England on June 28, 1929.

"He is rather forgotten today," wrote his friend E.M. Forster in 1944, "partly because he was a pioneer whose work has passed into our heritage."

ELEANORE ROOSEVELT

In the 1920s, many people loved to call Eleanor Roosevelt "ugly." Newspaper reporters gossiped about her fondness for wearing men's pants. J. Edgar Hoover's file on her mentioned love affairs with a black chauffeur, an Army colonel, a physician, and several National Maritime Union leaders. Hoover also called her an "old hoot owl," claiming he never married because "God made a woman like Eleanor Roosevelt."

The former first lady called Hoover "an old bastard and a fascist" when the rest of the nation stood ready to canonize him. She did not allow Hoover's criticisms of her to cramp her style, and she continued to pal around with her trousered lady friends. She also bought a little cottage early on in her marriage to Franklin. There she could gather privately with like-minded women to drink tea, host elaborate candlelight dinners, and read women's poetry. It was an atomsphere that made Eleanor happy because it afforded her opportunities to be "away from the men."

When Eleanor and Franklin first married, Franklin's mother persuaded him to buy two adjoining townhouses, one for the couple and one for herself. Shortly after they moved in, she began tearing down walls and adding doors. The two houses melded into one, making it easy for her to walk in on the couple unannounced and these walk-ins occurred with fearless regularity. (Biographers say the newlyweds were often caught in uncompromising positions, even though their marriage soon became a platonic partnership.)

Many people believe that Lorena Hickock was Eleanor's lesbian lover, the two having met sometime before 1932. Hickock was a journalist and very much in the closet. (She once chided a fellow female reporter for walking around in public with a copy of Radclyffe Hall's *The Well of Loneliness.*) Before Eleanor's move to Washington, the two often attended Broadway plays together in New York City. Historians speculate that after a speech at Cornell University, Eleanor may have confided in Hickock about her husband's affair with Lucy Mercer. Shortly after Eleanor's move to the White House, she began wearing a sapphire ring from Hickock.

Franklin's election separated the two women. Hickock remained in New York City, and the two began an intense correspondence. In these love letters, Eleanor declared, "Oh! How I wanted to put my arms around you in reality instead of spirit. I went and kissed your photograph..." Hickock wrote, "Goodnight, dear one, I want to put my arms around you and kiss you at the corner of your mouth."

A 1934 issue of (pro-Republican) *Time* magazine—in an obvious attempt to plant the seeds of a possible lesbian scandal—reported: "Miss Lorena Hickock, a rotund lady with a husky voice, a peremptory manner, and baggy clothes" was "a fast friend of Mrs. Roosevelt."

After Eleanor's death in 1962, Hickock arranged that the couple's correspondence be published ten years after her own death. Though the surviving letters are explicit, many were destroyed. (Lesbian-baiters have criticized Hickock's publication of the letters as a cheap desire to achieve posthumous fame.)

FDR let his wife do as she pleased. Then again, the male side of the Roosevelt family always had a quirky eccentric side. His father, whose first marriage was to an Astor, fathered a son who later became an auto mechanic. The mechanic lived a simple life in Queens and never touched his portion of the Astor fortune. He later willed the money to an organization that eventually became the Salvation Army.

An interesting aside: As acting secretary of the U.S. Navy, FDR established a vice squad to check "immoral conditions" at a naval training station. His officers botched the job when they enjoyed sex with the men before arresting them.

Little wonder that Eleanor sought refuges in her "female-only" cottage.

JAMES BALDWIN

Called "Baldly" in high school, the tagline under his yearbook photo had a prophetic ring: "Fame is the spur and—ouch!" Born in 1924, "life" for Baldwin began when he left Greenwich Village and his job as a waiter in an East Indian restaurant for Paris. These were the days when he was dubbed a "one-man force for integration." For instance, once he threw a mug at a waitress in a Trenton restaurant when told, "We don't serve Negroes here," whereupon a mob from the diner proceeded to chase him up the street.

To Baldwin, Paris was not only a place to write, it was an escape from American racial prejudice (he often called America "The Fourth Reich"). Once in France, however, he realized that discrimination and hatred were universal human flaws. The young writer starved in Paris, took odd jobs and lived on handouts from friends, including novelist Richard Wright. In Paris he rewrote *Go Tell It to the Mountain* (1953), which had been rejected by Harper's and two other publishers when he was in New York. After the revisions, he received a $1,000 advance from Knopf as well as eventual critical praise.

Returning to New York, he published *Giovanni's Room* ("Clumsy melodrama," said most critics.), a groundbreaking book about homosexuality. He would go on to write *The Fire Next Time* (1963), in which he takes a stand against violence and hatred of the white man as a means to correct racial injustice. Other books like *A Rap on Race* (1971) with anthropologist Margaret Mead were social consciousness tomes that critics said made Baldwin seem less of a literary figure, that he had abdicated the role of artist/novelist.

In New York and Paris, Baldwin found that fame often destroyed the solitude writing demands: late-night parties, countless visitors, and successions of young male lovers were things he struggled to regulate. Ironically, his Pentecostal roots (his preacher/stepfather called him "ugly frog eyes") and his childhood ambition to preach the gospel galvanized his passion for civil rights and social justice.

Many civil rights leaders, however, were embarrassed by Baldwin's homosexuality. His friendship with Martin Luther King, Jr. did not deter King and various civil rights leaders from preventing Baldwin's participation in the 1963 March on Washington. Eldridge Cleaver, the homophobic author of *Soul on Ice* (in which he compared homosexuality to baby rape and wanting to be president of General Motors), lashed out at Baldwin's "womanish" ways while insisting that homosexuality was racial genocide. Cleaver and more radical elements also called Baldwin an "assimilationist Uncle Tom," despite the fact that in later works Baldwin was considered by many to be "too extremist."

Despite these criticisms, Baldwin was sure that any commitment to hatred and bitterness was soul-destroying. Malcolm X experienced a similar revelation after a pilgrimage to Mecca, when he was able to see that the white man was not "the devil incarnate." Only then did the two men become friends.

Baldwin saw gay liberation as essentially a "white, middle-class phenomenon." He believed that what he did with another man was between himself and God. To him all people were basically androgynous or bisexual. "I do not have to join a club in order to go to bed with a man or fall in love," he said. Baldwin himself had many affairs with women, though a man, Lucien Happersberger, was the love of his life.

Baldwin was awarded the Commander of the Legion d'Honneur by François Mitterrand in 1986. After a diagnosis of throat cancer, he elected to spend his last days in bed in his mansion in France, where he had a superb view of the mountains. He died in 1987.

SAL MINEO

The fantastic rush of events in this, the first decade of the 21st century, has allowed us to forget minor celebrity, openly gay Sal Mineo, who was important for a number of reasons. First, he was an Italian-American actor who refused to change his name (or get a nose job to conform to Hollywood's cosmetic standards). Unlike Dean Martin (formerly Dino Crocetti), Mineo often proclaimed that he was "proud to be a wop."

"Italians ain't all olive-skinned," he told author Boze Hadleigh. "Look at Connie Stevens and Bernadette Peters."

Mineo was born in 1939 in New York. He landed his first film role, at 15, in *Six Bridges to Cross*, a film he later wanted to rename "Six Bridges to Burn."

"When I started in films," he said, "I had this baby face that made me look like a wheat-flour dumpling."

After *Bridges* came *Rebel Without a Cause*, with Mineo playing James Dean's brooding, love-struck friend, Plato. Mineo believed that Plato was the first gay teenager in films, and said: "You watch it now, you know he has the hots for James Dean." Mineo often hinted that he had an affair with Dean, though he said that Dean "was very often a shithead."

Other Mineo films included: *The Gene Krupa Story*, *Tonka*, and *The Longest Day*. He also worked with Paul Newman in *Somebody Up There Likes Me*, although he didn't get along with Newman, whom he said was on a star trip. Mineo said of him, "He's a great-looking ice cube." In *Exodus*, he played Cov Landau, a character who confesses that the Nazis used him "like a woman." "The word homosexual had hardly been mentioned in anything then, and when I said that...the speech, you could hear the shock."

He admired director Otto Preminger for helping to end movie censorship. "He was real anti-censor, pro-liberty," he said. "Years before *Exodus*, he was testing the censors with his subject matter.

Mineo could be very opinionated about his fellow actors. Charlton Heston's problem was "an ego the size of South Dakota." Jeffrey Hunter, who played Jesus in *King of Kings* was "young, bisexual, blue-eyed, gorgeous," and "a creep." In the Hadleigh interview, Mineo claims James Dean and actor Nick Adams were lovers, that Peter Lawford and he were lovers, and that actor Robert Taylor was a paranoid closet case who "put down gays and liberals in public." He also believed that bisexuality was the true norm for all men, and admitted that some of his relatives in Sicily were ragazzi di vita — hustlers. Never closeted about his sexuality, when he did *Fame* on stage, he came out to the public. He believed that *Fame* kept him from getting future roles, though he felt that "if the public sees you kiss a girl in a movie, that's what they remember, and that's what they assume.... If gay actors and stars and directors came out, that'll show the guys in charge that we're here."

Mineo said his Italian family accepted his sexuality as long as he didn't wear a dress or sound like Marilyn Monroe.

He was stabbed to death February 12, 1976, in front of his apartment building. At the time, he was working on the opening of *P.S. Your Cat Is Dead*, after a successful stage version of *Fortune and Men's Eyes*. His film career was over at the time of his death but he was experiencing a new life as a producer of plays. Like a recent Philadelphia murder case where the police were quick to say that a gay man died of erotic asphyxxiation/strangulation, L.A. police assumed that Mineo made a pass at a hustler and provoked his murderer, or that he died from kinky SM bondage games.

But the actor's killer was a thief who had no idea who Mineo was.

JAMES DEAN

After James Dean's death, Hollywood blurred the cult hero's homosexuality so that his rebel status might evoke the facile, revolutionary style of Elvis Presley.

Teenage boys may have emulated the actor's surly disposition, but lost on them was Dean's love of anonymous sex with men (a compulsion that made him late for studio calls), his visits to East Hollywood leather bars, and his fondness for dope and orgies. Dean may have broken the hearts of teenage girls when he posed beside Natalie Wood, but the true lights of his life were the various "Masters" who utilized him as, among other things, a human ashtray, crushing their lit cigarettes on his naked chest. "After his fatal car crash," wrote Kenneth Anger in *Hollywood Babylon*, "the coroner made note of the 'constellation of keratoid scars' on the actor's torso."

Dean did what many "smart" young actors did upon arriving in Hollywood; he hooked up with an older man, TV director Roger Brackett. Movie magazines at the time commented on the pair's father/son relationship, never daring to mention the obvious. At 22, Dean was no role model. Sources said he was friendless, suspicious, moody, rude. Directors humored him but cursed him behind his back. His temper tantrums were legendary. Once he threw a steak out of the window of Chasen's Restaurant while drinking with actor Tony Perkins. To get a waiter's attention he'd bang on glasses with forks or spoons. To reporters, he either talked in a make-believe dialect or said nothing at all. Anger noted that, "Dean betrayed a psychopathic personality, with fits of despondency that alternated with fits of wild jubilation—a classic manic-depressive—but his tormented screen persona hit a nerve with men and women."

At age 24, he made *East of Eden*, *Rebel Without A Cause* and *Giant* (which was released after his death).

Warren Beath said in *The Death of James Dean* that most of Dean's relationships were with women.

"He had never been part of the homosexual scene, except for a period when he was cravenly on the make with ambition. Enforced attendance at gay parties with an influential producer had left him with an aversion for the 'set,' so bound and constrained by their own codes of behavior."

But Anger said Dean was a "predatory night prowler who dug anonymous sex."

Beath linked Dean with women like Maila "Vampire" Nurmi, who starred in B movies like Ed Woods' *Plan Nine From Outer Space*. What both authors do not dispute is Dean's unflinching honesty in informing his Selective Service Unit that he was gay. Later, when Hedda Hopper asked him how he beat the draft, Dean replied, "I kissed the sergeant."

When actor Robert Francis (*The Caine Mutiny*) was killed in a plane crash on July 31, 1955, Dean said, "I'll be next."

The eve before he was killed, Dean was at a gay party in Malibu where he'd had a fight with an ex-lover.

The ex-lover accused him of dating women to enhance his public relations image. The following night Dean was riding in his two-week-old Porsche Spyder, on his way to a sports car race at Salinas, when he smashed into a 1950 Ford Tudor. Beath wrote, "Dean had been thrown backwards. He lay on his back, limp arms outstretched. His head hung sickening over the passenger door at almost a right angle."

Nine months after Dean's bronze headstone was erected at the cemetery in Fairmount, Indiana, it was stolen. Said Beath, "It was assumed that it had been taken by an obsessed fan. Some in Fairmount claimed to know it had been removed by an American Legionnaire outraged by a monument to any man who had evaded service in the armed forces by registering for the draft as a homosexual."

CARY GRANT

On screen, actor Cary Grant was the epitome of culture and class. In films such as *The Philadelphia Story, North by Northwest,* and *Arsenic and Old Lace,* he was, as New Yorker film critic Pauline Kael observed, "the ultimate dream date."

Off screen, Grant's four marriages were the result of a Paramount studio directive to "straighten" him.

Many biographers and film historians speculate that three of Grant's marriages went unconsummated. His last marriage, to Dyan Cannon, produced a child, although that relationship did little to affect the actor's attraction to men.

"Being married to him was hell," Cannon told the French magazine, *Hommes.* "He saw things only from his point of view. He was egotistical, and when high on LSD and booze, would fly into the most terrible rages and thrash me for no reason at all."

Born Archibald Alexander Leach in 1904 in Bristol, England, he became involved in the theater at age 6. At 16, he signed with The Penders, a troupe of traveling acrobats. The troupe traveled to New York by boat, and on the way, Grant had his first love affair with a man.

In New York, he met a female impersonator named Francis Renault. The two were lovers until the appearance of an Australian painter named Jack Kelly.

John Patrick, writing in *Legends,* said Grant appeared in many revues until he was discovered in 1925 by producer Jean Dalrymple. That same year, he was cast in a play called *Boom-Boom!* with Jeanette MacDonald. An affair during this time with composer Phil Charig created tension with Kelly. Grant's growing promiscuity also complicated matters. Patrick wrote that Charig called Grant's string of lovers his "kangaroo circle" — a circle that consisted of a dozen men.

Grant changed his name at the suggestion of actress Fay Wray when the two appeared in a play called *Niki.* At this time, he left Kelly and moved to Hollywood with Charig but the affair ended when Grant met Randolph Scott. The two moved to Santa Monica, California, where they hired a gay secretary and were the hosts of many wild all-male parties.

In 1942, Grant was arrested after an encounter with a young man in a department store men's room. Scandal was averted when the police were paid a huge bribe.

Grant's career attained national prominence after his role in Mae West's *She Done Him Wrong* (1933). By the time he starred in *The Awful Truth* (1937), he already was a member of Hollywood's super-elite.

Grant received two Oscar nominations before 1965, when he stopped making films. He died in 1986 at age 82.

JAMES MERRILL

In today's urban jungle, poetry is all the rage: poetry workshops, slams, open readings—everybody from street rappers to weekend bohemians are calling themselves poets. Media babble surrounding the craft is so intense it rivals Internet and cyberspace hype. No wonder so many want to shout, "Enough, already!"

James Merrill was a real poet. He didn't throw his body around in art galleries as jazz musicians caroused and painters painted "masterpieces" in arty settings. Merrill, in fact, hated the literary life with its book chat "professionals," petty jealousies and careerist chess moves. In 1954, after publishing his first poetry books, *First Poems* and *Short Stories*, he moved from New York City to Stonington, Connecticut with his lover David Jackson. The move was to prove beneficial. Stonington reminded Merrill of a Greek fishing village with its down-to-earth townsfolk, and he considered it the perfect place to concentrate on his craft. In 1959, he and Jackson bought a house in Athens, where they spent six months of each year.

Merrill was born in 1926 to Charles Merrill, the powerful financier of Merrill, Lynch fame "Merrill Lynch is bullish on America" was a famous advertising slogan for many years. He grew up on West 11th Street and began going to the Metropolitan Opera at age 11. His childhood was a rich and privileged affair. As a boy one of his favorite pastimes was operating a marionette theatre. At age 8, his father (taking time away from his many mistresses) had his son's poems analyzed by an academic panel to see if they showed promise. Told the work was good, he wasted no time publishing a private collection of his son's work, which became *Jim's Book*. "I would rather have a poet as a son than a third-rate polo-player," the poet's father said.

For the adult Merrill, opera was life's great teacher. Writing in *The New Yorker*, author J.D. McClatchy says that "Merrill would show up at the Met in later years in mauve Birkenstocks over lime-green socks, corduroys with a Navajo belt buckle, a shirt from the Gap, a loden cape, and a baseball cap."

In the late 60s, Merrill published *Nights and Days* and *The Fire Screen*. In these works he became concerned with the visionary and esoteric. The year 1976 saw the publication of "The Divine Comedies," in which the poet justifies his homosexuality by arguing that in avoiding procreation he is more like the angels. "The Divine Comedies" is part of a longer work, *The Changing Light at Sandover*, a 17,000-line epic that critics compare to Whitman's *Song of Myself*. Many critics insist that Merrill's epic is the grandest and strangest poem in American literature. The poem took its inspiration from an Ouija board experiment in which Merrill and Jackson talked with the spirits of Pythagoras, Maria Callas, T.S. Eliot, and W.H. Auden. ("Others crowd/About us. Wallace Stevens, dead that summer/Reads us jottings from his slate of cloud.") Most of Merrill's poetry can be seen as 'sacred books' in which the Ouija board is used as a source of divine intervention.

Some critics called Merrill's work "bejeweled." He was also criticized by poet W.S. Merwin for using the Ingram Merrill Foundation to award generous grants to (mostly handsome) young male poets and artists. Despite such charges, McClatchy claims that most in the poetry world feel that Merrill "knew more about the language of poetry than anyone since Auden," and that "not since a starry chapter closed in the 1970s with the deaths of Auden, Robert Lowell and Elizabeth Bishop has the loss of an American poet been as momentous."

Merrill, who wrote openly about gay love long before it was acceptable, died of a heart attack in Arizona in 1995.

ALEISTER CROWLEY

Toward the end of his life, mystic Aleister Crowley (a k a "the Great Beast") lived alone in London's Piccadilly Square, his body wasted from heroin and cocaine abuse—his great experiment in black magic and sexual hedonism, Thelema Abbey in Sicily, long fallen into ruin with its blood-drinking rituals and animal sacrifices.

Edward Alexander Crowley was born October 12, 1875, in Leamington, England, into a wealthy family that made its fortune in the brewery business.

Upon his father's death, Aleister inherited the family fortune and attended Cambridge, hoping to become a poet. In 1898, he joined the Hermetic Order of the Golden Dawn, an influential mystical society that taught that there are symbols familiar to all human beings, and that a person's actions and emotions can be manipulated by utilizing these symbols.

Golden Dawn was similar to the Masons with its systems of earned degrees and elaborate ceremonies. Members believed Lucifer to be a god of light, not the devil. They studied the tarot and attempted astral projection.

W.B. Yeats and Aubrey Beardsley belonged to the order. Bill Landis, author of *Anger: The Unauthorized*

Biography of Kenneth Anger, says this group formed "a cluster of competing egos, each trying to outdo one another." Beardsley thought Yeats a bore, while Yeats, disgusted by Crowley's bisexuality, dismissed "The Beast" as a "wild hooligan." Crowley later avenged himself by portraying the poet in his novel, *Moonchild*, as a shabbily dressed writer manipulated by black magic.

According to Landis, Crowley "enjoyed women not as sinless Madonnas, but as what he termed 'scarlet women.' He preferred highly intelligent, curious women with whom he could feel comfortable raising some hell."

Lawrence Sutin writes in *Do What Thou Wilt, A Life of Aleister Crowley*, that Crowley became involved with Dorothy Olsen, a striking Norwegian blonde with a "Garboesque profile" sometime after he met Jane Wolfe, a former Hollywood silent film character actress. Wolfe, who would become a lifelong friend of Crowley's, kept a diary in which she described several of her conversations with Olsen.

"On practically every occasion that I find myself alone with her she raved about A.C.; that in Paris he had tried to blackmail a former male lover...that in Sidi-bou-Said he had run around with Arab boys...."

Sutin writes that Olsen told Wolfe that an Arab boy had once come to her "weeping, saying, 'I don't want him! I want him to leave me alone!'"

Crowley was forthright in his defense of homosexuality and wrote: "Every one should discover, by experiences of every kind, the extent and intention of his own sexual universe. He must not be ashamed or afraid of being homosexual if he happens to be so at heart; he must not attempt to violate his own true nature because of public opinion, or medieval morality...."

With Leah Hersig, a Swiss woman, Crowley hung out in Greenwich Village and used heroin, cocaine and opium while dictating his writing to her. While sex, chess, mountaineering, hunting and drugs were his chief interests, Crowley still managed to create a huge body of work that once was difficult to obtain except in mimeographed form.

His book, *Diary of a Drug Fiend*, influenced writers such as Henry Miller and William S. Burroughs. "Like Cocteau and Genet," Landis wrote, "Crowley filtered his sexual experiences through erotica, much of it anonymous and privately produced."

Crowley's mystical works include *Magick in Theory and Practice* and *The Book of Law*, which satirized the Trinity and put down Jesus and Mohammed. In *The Book of Thoth*, published in 1944, Crowley designed his own tarot deck.

Sex researcher Alfred Kinsey, who once called Crowley "the most prominent fraud who ever lived," was fascinated none-the-less by Crowley's daily sex diaries, *King of the Royal Art*.

"The Beast's" decline began when the unsanitary conditions at Thelema Abbey caused some of his friends to die. His own baby was among the victims. After Crowley's death on Dec. 1, 1947, Kinsey and Kenneth Anger helped to "excavate" the abbey. Strangely, everyone connected with the cleanup died shortly after their visits (Kinsey included), the notable exception being Anger, who now lives in Palm Springs.

JILL JOHNSTON

How does one track down a lesbian writer who went into seclusion after her *Village Voice* column and published books made her famous in the 1970s?

With the tenacity of a detective, and the patience of a saint, thank you.

Not only couldn't the *Voice* tell me where their former colleague was living, they weren't even sure whether the author of *Marmalade Me* and *Lesbian Nation* (both anthologies of Jill Johnston's newspaper columns) was still writing and publishing. One editor did suggest contacting New York's Lesbian Herstory Archives — a lead which merely revealed that the outrageous '70s journalist was living somewhere in the country. Personal letters, the Archives clerk said, would be forwarded to Johnston provided they were enclosed, unsealed, in another envelope.

Unsealed, of course, meaning that that the contents would be inspected before being forwarded — a bad sign for a foe of censorship like myself.

Johnston's *Voice* column began as a commentary on dance but evolved into a stream-of-consciousness monologue about feminism and gay/lesbian New York once Johnston came out. With her long stringy hair,

Buddhist pendants, and denim outfits, Johnston was her own brand of radical lesbian feminist. Considered an outlaw by PC lesbians because of her distrust of political and activist groups, she also alienated mainstream feminists like Betty Freidan, who considered her a wacko. (Johnston, for her part, never criticized Freidan for her comment that the gay and feminist movements have nothing—and should have nothing—to do with one another.)

But Johnston's columns did succeed in making readers dizzy with their wild juxtapositions of both lesbian theory ("Feminists who still sleep with men are delivering their most vital energies to the oppressor."), and autobiography ("The reason I didn't stay Catholic is that I was certain I wanted women, so I went genealogical instead.").

Johnson's speech in May 1971 at New York's Town Hall created a major stir. Billed as a debate between feminist Germaine Greer and Norman Mailer (with Stephen Spender and Susan Sontag in attendance), Greer dragged Johnston onto the floor where they kissed and humped until the human tangle exploded in orgasmic moans. "Until all women are lesbians, there will be no political revolution," became "All women are lesbians"—all shouted by the participants during the staged exhibition.

"It was as if not one but three dykes in boots and overalls had come happily stomping into the wedding reception to eat all the cake and drink all the champagne," she said of the Town Hall affair in *Lesbian Nation*, mentioning also that the men in the audience booed her off the stage. Johnston obliged, perhaps heading for her favorite haunt, Max Kansas City, where she could see Andy Warhol, Tri-Grace Atkinson, or Yoko Ono.

Along with gay writer Arthur Bell, Johnston was one of the *Voice*'s few gay voices in the 70s. She wrote about her love affairs, or women she spotted necking in parked cars. At times she could be silly: "Lesbians are like upside-down cakes," but the topic of bisexuality brought out her serious side. "It [bisexuality] is not so much a cop-out," she wrote, "as a fearful compromise, the oppression of that part of the woman who would make it with another woman."

"Radical lesbians," she added, "know that men will not soon get better through the efforts of women to re-educate them."

Yoko Ono and John Lennon once sent her long-stemmed roses, books, patches and a bunch of shoes and socks.

I'm still waiting for Johnston's (sealed) reply.

NED ROREM

Pulitzer Prize-winning composer Ned Rorem is
certainly one of the most famous, openly gay
figures in the world of classical music. As the
author of seven operas, countless piano sonatas, songs,
and 12 published books, Rorem has described himself as
a "contradictory type...a radical by being a gay atheist,"
a "monarchist, in a way," a "Midwestern Quaker with a
WASP background," and a "composer who also writes,
not a writer who also composes."

Born in 1923, Rorem began composing music at
age 19 while a student at The Curtis Institute of Music.
After earning a master's degree at New York's Juilliard
School, he moved to Paris for eight years. He documented his time in France in the controversial *The Paris
Diaries* (1966), an infamous account of his promiscuous
sex life and adventures amongst Europe's moneyed and
artistic classes.

As an artist who's been out since the publication of
The Paris Diaries," and who has composed short musical
compositions on Sappho, Walt Whitman, and Marcel
Proust, Rorem confesses in his book, *Other Entertainment*, that it would be difficult to compose a homosexual
opera, that a full-length opera on the life of Walt Whitman or Marcel Proust—the two writers who fascinate

him the most—would be a thorny undertaking. Rorem takes this stance because he sees a sharp division between gay activism in life and gay activism or ideology implanted in music: not only would such operas risk being "too personal," but Rorem feels that such a marriage of art and ideology would be viewed as "propagandistic."

"Music, insofar as it's propagandistic, can never persuade," he wrote in *Other Entertainment*. "Insofar as it veers from propaganda, it can work...operas on racism, sexism, homophobia and AIDS would be too propagandist, too timely, to endure."

In his opinion, music does not have a sexuality, and that sexuality cannot be defined musically. "It can mean sad or happy, but nothing more specific: It can't mean green, or married, or cauliflower, or even quizzical or caustic."

Words, however, namely a libretto, can have a "sexuality," although Rorem believes the composer must be careful to see that the "long-range value of a piece goes beyond the theme that permeates it." That understood, a homosexual opera would then have to go beyond homosexuality, just as Rorem's piece on Paul Monette's *Elegies for Rog* for the New York City Gay Men's Chorus went beyond the subject of AIDS.

"It's not Whitman's homosexuality, but his universality that has made him beloved throughout the globe," Rorem wrote in *Other Entertainment*.

Homosexuality in itself is not an interesting subject for Rorem, "except insofar as it's a problem, and it's only made a problem by heterosexuals who make it one."

Rorem admits he's not much of a gay activist outside of the world of music composition, though he admires activists such as Larry Kramer. However,

Rorem can become his own brand of activist when confronted with blatant homophobia.

He took theater critic John Simon to task in 1985 for calling the play, *The Octette Bridge Club,* "faggot nonsense," and for publicly stating to actress Carrie Nye that he hoped "all the faggots in the theater world would get AIDS and die."

"The word 'faggot' offends homosexuals, take my word for it," Rorem told the New York Native in a joint interview with Simon. "...Use your freedom of speech instead to back up the solidarity of the few enough people who want to do something about AIDS research."

Rorem lives in Nantuckett, Mass. Musician James Holmes, his companion of several decades, died in the 1990s.

✦
PAUL GOODMAN
Teacher, Novelist, Radical Reformer

"I'm ever ready to play handball or make love or talk
with scholars." —P.G.

"There is no living American writer for whom I
have felt the same simple curiosity to read as
quickly as possible anything he wrote, on
any subject," wrote Susan Sontag on writer/social critic
Paul Goodman on the occasion of his death in 1972,

Born in 1911, Goodman was a teacher, poet, radical
social reformer, novelist and diarist. His *Growing Up
Absurd* was hailed by critics as the consummate sociological study of troubled youth, despite complaints that
Goodman talked about youth as if it were unique to
males alone. Goodman attributed the success of the
book to his homosexuality, which, he said, enabled him
to empathize with young men in a profound way.

In many respects far ahead of his time, Goodman
was usually at odds with New York and New Left intellectuals when it came to his sexuality. Ruthlessly honest
and out of the closet before it was either safe or chic (six
years before the advent of Gay Liberation), he braved

the slings and arrows of prejudice in the wake of having published his sexually explicit diary, *Five Years*.

"Until well into middle age, Paul's work was produced in poverty and against a blank of appalling neglect—and it poured out of him: poems, stories, plays, novels, literary criticism, works of psychology, community planning, social criticism, educational theory. He even composed some music. In his forty-ninth year *Growing UP Absurd* made him famous," wrote George Dennison in 1973.

Although he'd written twenty books by the time he was 46, he felt he never received the recognition he deserved, despite the fact that he influenced a whole generation of young people around the time of the Vietnam war.

Here was a social critic and poet, after all, who saw right through Jack Kerouac's *On the Road* when he bluntly stated that Kerouac's characters only pretend to rebel, that deep down they are boring and conventional because they never have homosexual experiences.

Goodman's pacifism and cantankerous attitude made him a unique curmudgeon. He smoked pot and had affairs with his male students at New York University. He participated in anti-war demonstrations and teach-ins. In one essay he advocated that cars be banned from mid-town Manhattan. A tireless champion of revolution in the mid-sixties, he called himself a "Utopian Socialist," as he urged twenty-year-olds to avoid the draft in essays like "We Won't Go" and "Designing Pacifist Films."

His stories and novels, such as *Adam and His Works*, *The Empire City*, and *Making Do* all have "out" gay themes that are still relevant today.

In the poem, "Long Lines: Youth and Age," Goodman wrote:

Like a hot stone your cock weighs on mine, young man,
And your face has become brutish and congested.
I'd draw back and gaze at it but drunk with carbon dioxide
We cannot stop snuffling each other's breath.

I am surprised you lust for a grayhead like me
And what a waste for me to grapple so much pleasure
With sliding palms holding your slim body
Firmly while you squirm, till it is time to come.

Come, lad...I have come with him for company
to his pounding heart. We are wet. Wistfully
I play with his black hair while he falls asleep
minute by minute, slowly, unlike my restless life.

It is quiet on his little boat. "He's a noisy lover,"
I notice idly – the April air is keen –
"but he has no human speech." It's I who say
the words like "I love you" or "Thank you."

Craggy-faced with black spectacles, Goodman's first wife left him in 1943, although he later remarried a woman named Sally. His one son, Matthew, was killed in a mountain climbing accident. To Matthew's memory he wrote "North Percy," probably the most moving elegy in American letters.

He was never one to cower from the truth of his homosexuality, whether in the classroom, in complex political situations, or brandishing about foolishly on the beach. (One time he was given a black eye when he told a guy's girlfriend to "get lost so me and your boyfriend can be men together.") *Five Years* (a diary a la Ned Rorem) also contains thoughts about God,

Thom Nickels

psychology, Goodman's Jewishness, and art. Though much of the sexuality in *Five Years* might be seen as obsessive/compulsive, Goodman frowned on heterosexual exclusivity and advocated an "experimental sexuality."

His eloquent essays against censorship and anti-pornography laws were written in 1951, before the rise of the McCarthy era. "...In cases relating to pornography," he wrote, "people apparently cannot simply leave off, for those laws and prosecutions are psychological means of keeping down their own confused panic."

"He was our Sartre, our Cocteau," Sontag wrote. "But he had gifts that neither Sartre nor Cocteau ever had: an intrepid feeling for what human life is about, a fastidiousness and a breadth of moral passion."

✦
LAWRENCE OF ARABIA

L awrence of Arabia's alcoholic father would not discipline him as a child, but his mother beat him often. One such beating occurred when she discovered young Thomas Edward Lawrence engaging in an act of mutual masturbation with another boy. Sometimes young Lawrence sought refuge from his mother's tyranny in a hut he constructed near the family house. As an undersized teenager who limped because of an ankle fracture, he eventually ran away and joined the Army, but was released eight months later by his father. Undeterred, this future "desert hero"—who would be made famous by journalist Lowell Thomas' idolatrous book about him after the British government demanded that Thomas produce a war hero to counter-act anti-British sentiment in America—joined the Army a second time.

Lawrence was instrumental in the British Empire's support of Sharif Hussein of the Hedjaz—and what one critic called "his charming sons"—during the Boer War. Fellow generals, however, insisted that he loved posturing in the limelight and dressing as an Arab. Others said he was nothing but a megalomanical Walter Mitty charlatan who'd invent lies about himself for notoriety's sake. Publicly, for instance, Lawrence claimed he loved barracks life and the company of men, when privately, he spoke disparagingly of the Army "low life."

Lawrence's critically acclaimed masterpiece, *Seven Pillars of Wisdom*, was said by biographer Lewis Aldington to be full of tall tales. Aldington wrote: "The propaganda which represents him as the shrinking victim of a notoriety thrust upon him against his will is just one more myth—of his own creation." Another biographer hailed *Seven Pillars* as a great work of art, but condemned *The Mint*, Lawrence's masochistic account of his life in the Royal Air Force. Notable among the stories is Lawrence's capture by a Turkish sultan who had him flogged and buggered by a number of men in his command. Lawrence himself had nine different versions of this story, and wrote that, during this beating at Deraa in 1917, a "delicious warmth, probably sexual, swelled through me." Some critics maintain this was the release of seminal fluid and that the psychosexual event marked the beginning of Lawrence's masochism.

Some historians theorize that despite Lawrence's homosexual orientation, he never acted on his queer impulses—that he prized his virginity and viewed sexual relations with loathing. That he had heterosexuality in mind when insisting he could never fall in love and didn't like to be touched, there can be no question. His relationship with Dahoum, the 15-year-old Arab donkey boy, was significant. Not only was *Seven Pillars* dedicated to Dahoum, but Lawrence wrote eloquently of homosexuality, refusing to see it as something his homophobic biographers called "a negative imputation." Once he mocked a heterosexual friend's passion for his young wife when he wrote that: "clean homosexual love ('friends quivering together in the yielding sand with intimate hot limbs in supreme embrace') was better than sordid affairs with women."

Lawrence befriended E.M. Forster, Winston Churchill, John Buchan and Robert Graves. With Forster, he exchanged writings on homosexuality. Robert Graves often spoke of the man's bright blue eyes, but added that: "they never met the eyes of the person whom he was addressing, but seemed to be making inventory of clothes and limbs."

Lawrence's penchant for sadomasochism included the employment of a 19-year old soldier to beat him daily on various parts of his body. Presumably, he was hoping for the same seminal release he experienced in the Turkish sultan's den. He died a heroic death in 1935 when he ran his motor scooter into a ditch, trying to avoid running down two boys on bicycles.

MALCOLM BOYD

In 1955, Malcolm Boyd, 31, a closeted gay man and a former TV and radio producer, was ordained a priest in the Episcopal Church. Because of his influential background, the occasion was marked by bright lights and television cameras. The day's celebratory mood faded to a dim memory, however, when Boyd's work as a priest exposed him to the hypocrisy and intolerance of the church he promised to serve.

In his essay, *Telling a Lie for Christ*, Boyd wrote: "The homophobia within this very structure...deeply shocked me as I gradually became aware of its hard reality. It was due to the self-hatred, the low esteem generated by closeted homosexuals who were both my leaders and my peers...I discovered cynicism, bitterness, frustration and considerable anguish."

To soothe his spirit, Boyd took long walks and meditated in the Arizona desert. He also slept with a number of other priests, although he preferred liaisons with waiters and cooks because the closeted priests were as paranoid about detection as he was. Today Boyd admits that, at that time, his spiritual life was in a shambles.

"Once a gay man was in love with me, and I with him," he wrote in *Telling a Lie*. "But I could no more have lived an open life with him—worked out a good relationship—than I could, under the circumstances, [have] rocketed to the moon."

Eventually, he was able to reconcile his homosexuality and spiritual life. The internal fusion was the result of an odyssey that took him halfway around the globe: to Taize, the Protestant monastic community in France, to the vermin-infested Greek Orthodox monasteries on Mount Athos, to the hermitage doors of Thomas Merton in Kentucky's Abbey of Gethsemani.

These experiences, as well as his time as rector of a slum church in Indianapolis, helped elevate his consciousness. Soon, he was getting involved with freedom rides to the South, where he marched with Martin Luther King Jr. in many demonstrations, including the 1968 nonviolent protest against the Vietnam War.

"King will stand as a more lasting figure in American history than any U.S. president who served in his lifetime," Boyd wrote in his memoir, *Gay Priest.*

Boyd was eventually able to experience "mutuality" in his relationships. In *Gay Priest*, he wrote of the importance of lovers not smothering each other, but "providing mutual space for various separate activities."

His 24 published books have garnered various reactions. *Playboy* called Boyd a "balding, battling Episcopal priest," while *The New York Times Book Review* branded him "a sort of balding Holden Caulfield become Episcopal priest."

Despite, or perhaps because of the hypocrisy of his closeted fellow clerics (he maintains that one-third of Catholic and Episcopal priests are gay), Boyd has continued to publish and lecture.

"Our creation in the image of God includes sex, as well as other aspects of our lives," he wrote in *Gay*

Priest. "Much so-called evangelism has exploited human fears, preached hate instead of love, espoused denial and repression in the place of fulfillment, and even heretically implied that one can earn salvation by the act of abstinence, rooted in legalism, instead of faith...."

Today, the Rev. Canon Boyd is poet/writer-in-residence at Los Angeles' Episcopal Cathedral of Saint Paul.

CHRISTOPHER ISHERWOOD
The Man Behind *Cabaret*

Christopher Isherwood was born in Cheshire, England, in 1904. He enrolled in Cambridge University but left before graduating to study medicine. He dropped medicine for literature, and in 1928 published his first novel, *All The Conspirators*, which was judged an artistic failure. He then moved to Berlin, where he spent four years gathering material for *Goodbye to Berlin* (later reissued as *The Berlin Stories*), which chronicled the life of his most famous fictional character, Sally Bowles. This book formed the basis of the movie, *Cabaret*.

Isherwood found life in Berlin more exciting than life in England. The city had few social and sexual constraints, so he was free to have love affairs with German boys. Isherwood occupied himself by giving English lessons every day and then going out at night with his boyfriends. "Berlin," he wrote, "was a very dark and drab city in the winter with heavy buildings. In its working class world, every attractive man was under economic pressure to become a hustler; nobody was getting enough to eat. These hustlers were apt to become gang-minded; they joined political parties which fought in gangs against other rival political gangs."

Though he never hustled for sex, Isherwood said he dressed like a hustler when he frequented Berlin's gay bars and cafes.

In a 1973 *Gay Sunshine* interview with Winston Leyland, Isherwood expressed annoyance at people who asked him if homosexuality had anything to do with the decadence of pre-WWII Germany. "It's such a vicious oversimplification to say that pre-Hitler Germany was decadent and so a Sodom and Gomorrah punishment fell upon it through the Nazis who in their run of course were decadent too."

In Germany, Isherwood met with Dr. Magnus Hirschfeld of the Institute for Sexual Science. Hirschfeld reeducated the German police and liberalized their attitudes on sex, though Hirschfeld's work (as well as the Institute's) was destroyed by the Nazis.

"I remember how Hirschfeld put on a special scientific demonstration for Andre Gide," Isherwood said. "Among other exhibits they brought in a boy with two perfectly-formed female breasts. Gide sat there judiciously holding his chin. He had a very pragmatic attitude toward the whole thing and didn't want to listen to a lot of theories. Gide liked very young boys. At the bar he visited they couldn't find anyone young enough for him, so they produced a boy who was actually 23 but looked 15." Gide struck Isherwood as being "rather grand and gracious, with a cape."

He thought Gide a snob, but only because Gide didn't live in the slums.

Isherwood emigrated to the United States with poet W.H. Auden in 1939 and became an American citizen in 1946. At that time he was drawn to the Quakers because of their pacifism and because of their positive views on homosexuality. He later moved to Santa Monica, California, where he began to write screenplays and to study Indian philosophy. He translated the Bhagavagita (with Swami Prabhavanada) and later wrote *Ramakrishna and His Disciples.*

He met 18-year old photographer Don Bachardy when he was in his 40s. Bachardy became his lover and companion until Isherwood's death in 1986.

"The combination of sex and friendship," he once wrote, "can be beautiful but it's apt to be short-lived because excitement doesn't last when you feel the awareness of likeness. The love remains, but it's a different kind of love. How could you fall in love with someone about whom you could say, 'He's exactly like me?' That would be sheer narcissism."

MARGUERITE
RADCLYFFE-HALL

Marguerite Radclyffe Hall was born in 1886 in Bournemouth, England. Educated at London's King College and in Germany, at the time of her death in 1943, she had published four volumes of poetry and many novels, including *The Well of Loneliness* (1928), a sympathetic study of the lesbian experience. The book's publication resulted in a notorious obscenity trial that banned the book in England for several years.

Marguerite's father, Radclyffe-Radclyffe Hall, was a handsome, independently wealthy poet/dandy who spent his life traveling and having love affairs. He married Mary Diehl of Philadelphia, a silly, jealous woman with a vile temper, according to biographers. The marriage ended in divorce, leaving Marguerite in her mother's care. After the death of her father, Marguerite, having inherited his vast estate, became a very wealthy woman indeed—free at last to grow her blond hair down to her waist, dress in men's clothing, walk with a swagger and smoke little green cigars.

Shortly after the publication of her first book of poetry, *Twixt Earth and Stars*, Marguerite met her first lover. Mabel Batten, an Irish beauty noted for her sophistication, took the young poet under her wing and taught her to accept her homosexuality, to reject society's notion that it was an "ugly affliction."

Marguerite, who now called herself John, became a Catholic under Batten's influence. Batten also sent John's short stories to William Heinemann, a London publisher. "I am not going to present you to the public as a writer of a few short stories," Heinemann told the author. "You will set to work at once and write me a novel, and when it is finished I will publish it." Eleven years later, John's first novel, *The Forge*, was published to mixed reviews. About this time, John met sculptor/artist Una Troubridge, the wife of a prosperous admiral. The two women fell in love, causing a painful (and eventually fatal) rift between John and Mabel—for during a discussion about Una, Mabel lapsed into unconsciousness and died of a cerebral hemorrhage.

Torn by guilt, John turned to a medium, Mrs. Osborne Leonard of London, to communicate with Mabel's spirit. Her work with Mrs. Leonard coincided with John's interest in The Society for Psychical Research, an organization dedicated to the study of thought transference and the appearances of ghosts. (Poet W. B. Yeats, also a member, conducted séances.) When Mrs. Leonard told John that Mabel had forgiven her, life with Una was at once more pleasant.

John's success as a novelist (*Adam's Breed* won the prestigious Tait Black Memorial Prize) mushroomed when she published *The Well of Loneliness*, though a host of publishers rejected the manuscript before Jonathan Cape published a limited edition. The book's notoriety caused John to become an international celebrity. In America, The Society for the Suppression of Vice declared that the book's subject matter was taboo; on

January 12, 1929, *The New York Times* reported that the book had been seized by the police.

John and Una endured normal marital problems until John met Eugenia Souline, a nineteen-year-old Russian immigrant. The two women had a passionate affair, which ended just before John became ill with eye ulcers and abdominal tumors.

"...What one remembers," wrote Hall biographer Lovat Dickson, "is not that fierce affair, but the flame burning steadily and faithfully in the 'single soul' of Una Troubridge."

John died of cancer on October, 7, 1943.

JOHANN JOACHIM WINCKELMANN

Johann Joachim Winckelmann (1717-1768), one of the greatest scholars of the 18th century, was born in Prussia to a poor cobbler and had many false starts in life—first as a penniless theology student at the University of Halle, and then as a student of medicine at the University of Jena.

Young Winckelmann detested his formal education and left his medical studies when a blind rector at a Lutheran church asked him to be his personal reader. The serendipitous appointment helped him fulfill his destiny as the creator of art criticism and inspirer of modern archaeology, subjects Winckelmann familiarized himself with by studying Greek texts and voracious reading.

In 1745, he acquired a teaching post at a village school near Seehausen, where he taught children to read and write. He was 23 at the time and living with one of his male students, Peter Lamprecht, with whom he fell in love. The unrequited affair plunged him into despair, as did his near-romance with another indifferent youth named von Bulow. Another ill-fated match with a Baltic baron, Fredrich von Berg, inspired A.L. Rowse to write in *Homosexuals in History* that "Lamprecht and von Berg would never have been heard of, except that a man of genius once fell for their looks when they were young."

By 1748, Winckelmann, well into his life as a neoclassical scholar and antiquarian, was appointed librarian to a Prussian count who lived near Dresden. This post taught him to consolidate his readings in classical literature. In Dresden, he met Cardinal Passionei and became his personal librarian. As the cardinal's sidekick, Winckelmann studied fine paintings and deepened his knowledge of Greek literature, upon which his interpretation of Greek art was based.

Winckelmann began to publish essays on art, beauty, and Italian architecture. Extraordinarily, these works, based on his own readings, were created outside any university setting. Works like *Essay on the Beautiful Art* would influence giants like Goethe and win Winckelmann the title of most important scholar in Europe at that time.

In 1764, he published his masterpiece, *History of Ancient Art*, one year after he was installed as prefect of antiquities at the Vatican. To obtain the appointment, he felt it necessary to convert to Catholicism (he had been a Lutheran). Winckelmann was anything but an orthodox religionist, but he knew that a political conversion would give him access to Rome's collection of classical antiquities. In his new position, he met the cosmopolitan aristocrat, Cardinal Albani, who had none of the middle class prejudices against homosexuality and enjoyed hearing about Winckelmann's love affairs with Italian men. According to Rowse, Winckelmann once wrote: "I have found someone with whom I can speak of love; a good looking, blond young Roman of 16, half a head taller than I am." Rowse also reports that Winckelmann had affairs with a number of young Florentines.

Biographers, including Rowse and David Irwin, allude to Winckelmann's open and sanguine nature, a personality trait that undoubtedly led to his befriending an ex-criminal while traveling through Italy. Both men had traveled together for several days when Winckelmann mentioned some gold and silver medals he'd received in Vienna. Music to his ears, the thug demanded the medals at knifepoint as Winckelmann, defending himself, tripped on some furniture. He was stabbed twice, after which the murderer fled without taking the medals or any money.

GORE VIDAL
Rejects the Term, 'Homosexual'

As a young man, writer Gore Vidal was interviewed by sex researcher Alfred Kinsey in New York's Astor Hotel. World War II had just ended, and soldiers were flooding the Astor to meet other men for sex.

"In the war, just about everyone...was available under the right circumstances...", Vidal recalls in his memoir, *Palimpsest*. Although the traditional hysteria about same-sexuality ran its usual course in the well-policed Army camps Stateside, bars like the one on the ground floor of the Astor throve..."

Vidal always has maintained that there's no such thing as "a homosexual."

"I don't believe in the category," he told *Gay Sunshine* in 1974. "Only in a very sick, sectarian country like the United States would you draw two teams, the good straight team and the wicked gay team. To allow yourself to be categorized is to allow yourself to be enslaved..."

Vidal believes a person's primary attraction is innate and unchangeable, but that secondary attractions are possible.

"Hence the tradition, in patriarchal societies, of a conventional marriage for Jonathan as well as one for David, though their love for each other is the primary fact of their lives," Vidal is quoted in the *Gay Sunshine* article.

For years following the release of *The City and the Pillar*, The New York Times refused to review Vidal's books. To this day, Times reviewer Orville Prescott will not review anything Vidal publishes. The mysteries Vidal wrote under the Edgar Box pseudonym had been given glowing reviews by The Times but were reclassified as mediocre works once Vidal was revealed as their author.

Vidal prefers the term "same-sexualist" to either "gay," "homosexual" or "queer." The word he most admires is "faggot."

"I have never allowed actively in my life the word 'gay' to pass my lips," he told Boston's Fag Rag in 1973.

Vidal was born in 1925, and attended Phillips Exeter Academy. He joined the Army in 1943. After the publication of his first novel, *Williwaw*, he became known as a promising postwar writer. His literary output to date consists of 22 novels, five plays and numerous books of essays. Vidal always has put down as superstition the Hemingway model of maintaining continence while working. He writes best, he told Fag Rag, when he's sexually promiscuous.

For more than 30 years, Vidal shared his life with Howard Austen in Ravello, Italy. Their relationship remained platonic until Austen's death in 2003.

"Where there is no desire or pursuit, there is no wholeness. But there are satisfying lesser states, fragments," he writes in *Palimpset*.

In his memoir he confesses: "You don't live with the person you love. You live with a friend, which is something quite different from having a grand passion...."

WWII killed Vidal's grand passion, Jimmie Trimble, a 19-year-old he met at Exeter. At 77, Vidal admits to being "possessed" by Trimble "in fading present time."

AN EVENING
WITH GORE VIDAL

When a friend and I heard that Gore Vidal was going to be speaking at the New York Society for Ethical Culture on West 64th Street, we reserved our tickets weeks in advance. The talk was billed as a conversation with WNTC's Leonard Lopate and sponsored by The Nation Institute (a.k.a. *The Nation* magazine, or to my mind, the only political publication worth reading in America).

Ordinarily robust and dynamic, Vidal, in his late 70s, is partially lame and his eyes have the look of someone not in good health. We figured, sadly, that this might be our last chance to see America's greatest living writer. Having seen a documentary about Vidal's life at a recent Philadelphia Film Festival, we knew that Vidal and his companion of many decades, Howard Austin, had sold their villa in Italy and were already living in Los Angeles before Austin's death in late 2003.

Vidal had decided to move back to America, but why? My astute friend speculated that Vidal chose Los Angeles because it has the best physicians in the world. Vidal's Hollywood connections may also have been a draw. First and foremost, my friend ventured, Vidal wanted to be close to America again after more than several decades of living abroad. "He wants to live here because of what has happened in this country. He wants to join the fight against the Bush-Cheney junta and help lead a charge for a new American revolution."

Out of the villa, into the streets.

The New York conversation, which was to begin at 7 p.m., had already drawn a long line down 64th Street by the time we arrived at 5:45. It was a particularly hip Manhattan crowd: students, bearded professor types, matrons in long earrings, and well-heeled couples who looked as though they would be attending the $125-a-plate dinner with Vidal at *The Nation*'s Victor Navasky's townhouse after the talk.

Happily, we were seated in the fourth row by 6 p.m. Not a bad seat at all considering all the poor souls who were relegated to the balcony.

Mention Vidal to different people and you get different reactions. Commercial banker types might insist he's a pompous ass. Social reactionaries loathe him. A learned Christian gay friend of mine in Boston once called him a pagan.

Certainly an iconoclast and a provocateur, in the late 1970s Vidal infuriated a rather conservative Barbara Walters, who used to make snide remarks to Vidal about his homosexuality. When changing times later "dictated" that it was okay to be gay, Walters changed her tune. (Allow me, but...as an interviewer, Walters has never been *ahead* of the curve.)

Vidal, who has a predominately straight reader-ship—an unusual thing for a "gay writer," even if he insists that gay is an adjective and not a noun—crossed the bridge into the literary mainstream years ago with historical novels like *Burr, Lincoln, 1876,* and *Justinian.* What other internationally known gay writer can claim such a huge non-gay readership? Truman Capote, at one point, maybe, and ditto for Tennessee Williams, but in today's world, Vidal stands alone. Almost all of the out gay writers today write gay fiction for gay audiences. No one, not even the eclectic Edmund White, has cultivated as wide and diverse an audience.

In the lecture hall, seated barely ten feet away from us, there appeared one Dick Cavett and his wife, actress Carrie Nye. I noticed Nye first, her long blond hair framing a face quite different looking than the "Palmolive" one that I remembered as a teen. Cavett, who left the world of television due to a series of nervous breakdowns — serious affairs that caused the cancellation of his recent cable TV show (Cavett announced that he just couldn't do it, and quit) — had a pained expression on his face, although he was still unmistakably Dick Cavett.

We spotted at close range former Senator George McGovern and his wife. McGovern entered an aisle across from us and moved in a slow and dignified manner, his rustic face somehow reminiscent of Lincoln's with its gray, ashen solemnity. Richard Nixon slaughtered McGovern in the 1972 presidential race, but did the country make the right choice then? Is the country making the right choices now?

Just two hours before, seated on an outdoor bench at the Trenton train station waiting our connection into the city, my friend and I had spotted another politician, traversing the platform with two other people. Her bobbed, short blond hair iridescent in the afternoon light, announced that she was the ex-Governor of New Jersey, Christie Whitman.

Whitman's toothy smile is something to see. I tried not to stare but since she was only several feet from me I could not help but eyeball her in what I thought was a discrete fashion until I noticed her taking quick peeks at me before moving behind a platform column when she thought I wasn't looking. She was schmoozing with an Amtrak cop who had come to the platform to guard her, as well as an Amtrak PR woman with long frizzy hair and big Jackie O sunglasses. I kept imagining George Bush shaking her hand or patting her on the shoulders in the cold junta rooms of the White House.

I checked out her shoes: an updated brown and white Buster Brown combination, strictly Republican chic with a junta heel.

She was, obviously, on her way back to Washington. I watched as she took periodic looks over the side of the track as if looking for something amiss. A rat? A terrorist?

Nation editor, Katrina vanden Heuvel, in her introductory remarks at the Vidal event, compared the Bush administration to a regime of the worst despots — or rats.

When Vidal appeared onstage he had to be helped into his chair. He began by reading a statement and pointing out McGovern's presence in the audience. Vidal's talk was mainly political. He said that the silent takeover in America began with the partisan Supreme Court ruling in Florida in 2000 that appointed Bush president. There were no huge protests then, he said, no uprising. The junta came into power without a struggle.

There is no free press in America, he continued: the corporate-controlled broadcast media, with its stories of war heroes, is utterly hopeless, and the print media is only marginally better. He did have some "good" news to share, however: that Bush's popularity will crumble once the economy forces Americans to look beyond their pretty patriotic yellow ribbons. That theatrical patriotism will give way once this nation is in financial ruins.

After a standing ovation, Vidal left the stage and that was that.

Vidal had come to New York primarily to promote his book, *Dreaming War, Blood for Oil and the Cheney-Bush Junta* (Nation Books). *Dreaming War* is an intense but short overview of America's fall from Republic to Empire, but lest you think that the crumble began with the Cheney-Bush Junta, think again. "I am a patriot of the old Republic that slowly unraveled during the expansionist years and quite vanished in 1950 when the National Security State took its place. Now I want us to convert from wartime to a peacetime economy. But since the GE-style conglomerates that govern us will never convert, something will have to give, won't it?" he asks.

Vidal says that America's golden age lasted from 1945 to 1950, when the arts flourished. Behind the scenes, however, "the managers of the new world empire were hard at work replacing the republic for which we had fought with a secret National Security State, pledged to an eternal war with communism...." FDR baited the Japanese, he writes, and so the attack on Pearl Harbor was not unprovoked. President Truman ignored a letter from the Japanese Emperor seeking peace, opting instead, Vidal asserts, to "intimidate the Soviets with our super-weapon."

The truth gets even uglier as Vidal writes that after WWII Americans had the highest personal income taxes in the history of the country, all to fight a Cold War that was mainly the creation of the nation's managers, not the American people. He even dares to ask how great the greatest nation on earth actually is, in lieu of the fact that "We have no health service or proper public education or, indeed, much of anything for the residents of the fun house," he is quick to point out.

Vidal has always been a prophet of doom and sometimes his most dire prophecies have a Nostradamus-like ring. In *Dreaming War* he refrains from shocking predictions but manages to back up most of what he says with facts and figures.

In the book, Vidal hints at Bush's inevitable impeachment—perhaps his most Nostradamus-like prediction—and comes down hard on events surrounding Sept. 11, 2001, on what Vidal calls "the complicit behavior of George Bush on 9/11."

Items in Vidal's brief include: that George Bush Sr. works for the bin Laden family business in Saudi Arabia (the Carlyle Group), that he has met with the bin Laden family at least twice in the past, that Taliban representatives were invited to Sugarland, Texas, and that Condoleeza Rice's old employer was Chevron Oil. The plot gets thicker and the facts tumble out faster than Myra Breckinridge twirled her baton back in Vidal's days of carefree fiction.

But Gore Vidal's allegations do not stop there. He firmly believes that Americans—innocent and ignorant Americans—are being hoodwinked by yellow ribbons, Support Our Troops rhetoric and patriotic prattle, in a governmental effort to divert attention away from the reality that the wars in Afghanistan and Iraq were nothing but "an imperial grab for energy resources."

Will Americans wake up? Vidal believes so. "Mark my words," Vidal writes, putting his predictive powers on the line once again. "[Bush] will leave office the most unpopular president in history. The junta has done too much wreckage."

Here's to hoping that this time the Nostradumus in Vidal hits a home run.

YUKIO MISHIMA
The Last Samurai

In Japan, samurai families honored the code of absolute control over mind and body; they also expected loyalty to the Emperor.

Novelist Yukio Mishima's birth in 1925, into a prominent samurai family, assured him certain privileges. He had a domineering grandmother and a doting mother, both of whom fought for his attention—in the process, helping the boy to become a delicate, spoiled prima donna. As an adult, this personality trait led to Mishima's highly specialized erotic tastes: he would only make love with muscular men with flashing white teeth. Nothing else would do for the persnickety prince.

Mishima (a pen name suggested by a teacher) wrote and published his first "novel" in a school magazine when he was 13. In 1941, his first story, "The Forest in Full Bloom," appeared in a commercial magazine. Later, a collection of short stories was published under the same title. He attended Tokyo Imperial University, and as a student became familiar with Tokyo gay literary circles, as well as Tokyo's many gay bars. (Gay bars in Tokyo are so small they can barely hold six people). Duty-bound to the demands of conventional family life, however, Mishima followed the wishes of his parents and consented to an arranged marriage.

In *Confessions of a Mask*, an autobiographical novel, Mishima tells the age-old tale of a homosexual living a double life. The book won him recognition as a writer. In *Forbidden Colors*, a misogynistic work according to most critics, Mishima is forever criticizing feminine influences.

"Everywhere you look," one character says, "feminine instincts win out. What a waste it is that man insists on being attracted by woman! What disgrace it brings down upon man's spiritual powers!"

"Women's jealousy," another character says, "is simply jealousy of man's creativity."

He took up bodybuilding in 1955 and created a superb body that he refused to see decay. He studied kento (fencing with bamboo sticks) in 1959, and later, karate. Despite his powerful physique, the masterful novelist didn't know how to swim or drive a car. As A.L. Rowse notes in his essay on Mishima, "he was erotically excited by a portrait of the torture of Saint Sebastian and loved sexual excitement in torture, violence, blood and death."

His private army of 100 young men differed from the usual right-wing organizations in that it did not engage in violence or military action. Nor was it ever monitored by the Japanese police. It was, as one writer put it, "more a theatrical fantasy conceived by a poet."

"In Japan, there has always been a respected homosexual element in samurai tradition as in ancient Greece," writes Rowse. Though extremely work obsessed (his literary output consists of over a hundred books, including 15 novels), he could often be a creature of impulse, as when he flew to the United States one weekend to cruise for a perfect Caucasian male with flashing white teeth.

Critics compare Mishima's works to the works of Gide and Proust and write of his obsession with courage and "manly" virtues. After the completion of his tetralogy, *The Sea of Fertility*, the author confessed to friends that he felt useless, having put everything he felt about life into the work.

Feelings of nihilism were nothing new to Mishima. From his youth he often told friends that he wished to die young. His poetic vision included dying at the peak of his physical beauty, untouched by age and decay.

On November 25, 1970, he committed seppuku, or ritual suicide, at 45 years of age.

FREDERICK II,
KING OF PRUSSIA

Frederick II, King of Prussia (1712-1786) became known as Frederick the Great after transforming a mediocre German state into a great European power.

As a child, he had to deal with an ogre of a father, Frederick William I, who suffered from a hereditary disturbance of the metabolism. This caused him to experience delirium, tremors, depression and schizophrenia, resulting in abusive and erratic behavior. Often he would castigate subjects who feared him with comments like, "It's your duty to love me, scum bag!" He also had a habit of kidnapping big-boned, slow-witted men for his guard, though his worst abuses were directed towards his son, whom he perceived as overly delicate and refined. He forbade the boy to study poetry, philosophy, literature and Latin, and often abused and humiliated him in public.

Nancy Mitford, in her biography of Frederick the Great, described him as a "particularly thin and beaky boy whose face seemed to contain only two enormous blue eyes — dazzling as the sun." Unfortunately, young Frederick's personality drove his father into a state of sadistic frenzy. The son lived in such fear of his father that he often went to extraordinary lengths to please him, such as kissing his feet in public.

Tired of his father's manipulation and beatings, Frederick tried to escape to England with two friends, his lover, Lieutenant Hans Hermann von Katte and a boy named Keith. Only Keith managed to escape, but von Katte and Frederick were imprisoned and immediately court marshaled. Frederick William, who had always objected to the intimate friendship between von Katte and his son, now had legal recourse to order the Lieutenant's execution, a decapitation he forced his son to watch, even though Frederick begged to be killed in place of his friend. It's said that when von Katte went to the scaffold, Frederick "blew a kiss from the window of his cell and shouted repeated pleas for forgiveness."

"As the sword fell," wrote Frank Richardson in his study *Some Homosexual Generals*, Frederick fainted, but revived to see the body lying beside the blood-soaked pile of sand, which he was convinced was awaiting the head of the next victim—his own."

Just as Frederick was about to be led to the scaffold, his father offered him a reprieve, a move he engineered to "soften" the boy into deeper submission. Indeed, Frederick was so happy to be spared death, he wrote his father an abject letter of submission.

There was little love in Frederick's life after the death of von Katte, and he spent most of his time waiting for his father to die. In the meantime, he was forced to go through with a pre-arranged marriage. After the ceremony, he banished his wife to separate quarters and only saw her once or twice a year at formal functions. "There can be neither love nor friendship between us," he told her.

Once his father died, he was able to establish an all-male court and became friends with Voltaire, making the philosopher writer-in-residence and giving him a large apartment near his own. This friendship lasted a couple of years but eventually the two men had a falling out. Voltaire had been put into the odd position of having to admire the writing of a king who desired to be a great author in the 'French literary tradition' but who had no talent for writing. It seems the great French author/philosopher was no good at faking admiration when he really felt otherwise.

Frederick was, however, a great military organizer and an imposing commander. He also abolished press censorship, torture, and championed intellectual interests. His primary fault was a cruel tongue; he'd often lash out at people for no apparent reason. No doubt this behavior had its roots in the psychological damage inflicted by his father.

NAPOLEON BONAPARTE

Napoleon Bonaparte's small stature and his seductive power over women are two myths that need clarification: Napoleon was tall (5'6") compared to the average European male of 1800. He was also, as Major-General Frank Richardson writes in *A Study of Some Homosexual Generals,* "a misogynistic boor whose almost unbelievable public rudeness to women is well documented." His inhuman megalomania, according to psychologist Alfred Adler, sprang from a deep sense of social and "organ inferiority." German psychologist Wilhem Stekel put it bluntly when he compared the Emperor's "hypertrophic ambition" with his "strikingly small, infantile, undersized genitals," revealed at his postmortem examination. This Corsican with a dark olive complexion also spoke and wrote French badly and was so ashamed of his Latin heritage that he dropped a "u" from Bonaparte to give it an authentic French flavor.

Hailed by giants like Hegel, Goethe and Beethoven as the Messiah of a new order in Europe, the youthful Napoleon wrote diatribes against his military school classmates for pursuing girls in his only novel, *Clisson et Eugenie* (a work he dedicated to one of his mistresses). He had two wives, Josephine de Beauharnais and Marie

Louise. His marriage to Josephine ended in disillusionment. Despite her legendary sexual talents, as well as claims that she was "really a prostitute" (to quote Frank Richardson), the marriage was so infused with hatred that Josephine was reported to have rejoiced upon hearing false reports of Napoleon's death in Egypt.

The Emperor's legendary impotence made him the subject of rumor and innuendo. Women scoffed and political enemies taunted him about his "non-gendered/intersex" persona. Once the mother of a Russian grand-duchess he was courting called him "a man who could do nothing because he was not as other men," and "He keeps his balls in his head" was a common refrain throughout Europe at the time. Before age 36, he had a slender build with curly hair and a hawk-like nose. He later contracted Frohlich's Syndrome, which causes degenerative changes in the pituitary gland. The disease so transformed his features that he came to resemble a corpulent and elderly governess. Exiting from his bath one day, Napoleon boasted, "Breasts plump and round—any beauty would be proud of a bosom like mine!" states Richardson.

His enemies (especially the English) used his tolerance of homosexuality as opportunities to accuse him of "sexual deviation." Napoleon did tolerate widespread homosexuality among his troops in Egypt, and once said, "sodomy was the great vice of great men of old," according to Richardson. He also had a childhood friend who lived a very "out" homosexual life in Paris. As Emperor, he was fond of caressing a young soldier's earlobes, or pinching their noses. "Men, women and children were slapped, pinched and had their ears and noses pulled, often until blood was drawn. In his entourage there was no lack of men in their early twenties to be spanked, and to have their ears and noses pulled," writes Richardson. Napoleon understood the homosexual phase of a boy's life when, writing about one of his brothers at age 13, he says, "He loves his friend as he will love his mistress at twenty." He often took handsome drummer boys and made them subalterns in the Consular Guard, and his brief and passionate courtship of Tsar Alexander I of Russia began when he spotted Alexander on a raft on the Niemen River and shouted, "It is Apollo!" His chief aide-de-camp was Geraud Christophe-Michel Duroc. This intimate relationship lasted fifteen years and ended only with Duroc's death. Indeed, Duroc's tomb—not Josephine's—is next to Napoleon's in the Hotel des Invalides.

NICHOLAS SENSION

In colonial America, the usual penalty for sodomy was death. New Haven's anti-sodomy statute was the most severe: male-female anal intercourse, female "crimes against nature," and masturbation being cited as "crimes" that merited capital punishment.

In Pennsylvania, the Quakers (William Penn) abolished the death penalty for sodomy in 1682. In 1718, Pennsylvania reinstated the death penalty for sodomy and buggery but finally abolished the death penalty for the "crime" in 1786.

One of the most colorful "sodomitical characters" of the 1600s was Nicholas Sension. Sension came to America from England in 1640 and settled in Windsor, Connecticut. In 1645, he married a woman named Isabell. The couple remained married for life but had no children.

Sension distinguished himself by becoming one of the very richest residents of Windsor. He was a respected gentleman who gave regularly to the poor and who employed disadvantaged teenage boys to work for him as servants. Working for Sension assured the boys of a good life, a free education, and, it would seem, nightly bedroom visitations from their employer.

For over thirty years, Sension propositioned numerous young men not only as they lay sleeping but as they worked in fields, barns or haystacks. His long-term survival in colonial America, where a sodomy conviction equaled death, was a kind of miracle, even though his wealth and social status protected him in many ways.

In 1672, a youth named Daniel Saxon reported to the authorities that he saw Sension attempt to commit sodomy on Nathaniel Pond, 17. Court proceedings against Sension then produced lists of boys Sension had approached. The roll call reads like a page from Walt Whitman's Daybooks, in which Whitman listed the names and ages of young men he met in Philadelphia and Camden. But Sension lacked Whitman's gentle approach; even by today's standards, his cruising style can only be described as reckless.

Teenager George Griswald said that in 1646 he was in a mill house with Sension when "he took me and threw me on the chest and took hold on my privy parts."

Nathaniel Pond, a passionate favorite of Sension, complained to his brother Issac about his master's "sodomitical advances." Issac offered to take Nathaniel away, but the boy refused. Pond eventually learned to enjoy Sension's caresses, as various friends of Pond's noted in court. Some testified they saw Sension put his hand "to Nathaniel Pond's breech," or creep into Nathaniel's bed, whereupon the bed began to creak and shake.

Jacob Gibbs, also 17, said that Sension tried to hug him, "reaching his hands within my breeches, laboring to handle the lower part of my body in an uncomely manner." Farmboy Josiah Holcombe said he was lured to a haystack "where he Sension did endeavor to untie my breeches." Samuel Barbos testified that Sension offered him a bushel of corn if he'd pull down his breeches, and gun-loving Peter Buoll was offered a charge of powder for "one blow at his breech." Johnny Parsons said that Sension "clapped his hands about me and unbuttoned or unclasped my breeches." Daniel Saxon told the court that Sension turned him on his belly and kissed him "on the tail." A servant confirmed seeing Saxon in bed with Sension, and said: "I heard a rocking bed, and afterwards I saw Sension wipe something off Daniel."

In the 1600s, two witnesses were required before a person could be convicted of sodomy. Since only one witness could be found in Sension's case, he was charged with "attempted sodomy" and not punished. "American colonists," Jonathan Katz writes, "were sometimes more tolerant of sodomy (and attempted sodomy) than their still harsh legal codes implied."

Architect
PHILIP JOHNSON

One of the most celebrated architects of our time is an openly gay man who, at the time of this writing, is almost 95 years old. Philip Johnson was a delicate, effeminate child with four siblings and unaffectionate parents, all of whom he'd later dismiss as "irrelevant." The product of a privileged, if unhappy, upbringing, while still a Harvard undergrad, his father gave him Alcoa stock shares, which made young Philip a millionaire. As a result, he was able to employ butlers in his various student apartments throughout his Cambridge career.

Before Johnson became an architect at age 34, he was an architecture critic who made a name for himself when he arranged the historic 1932 International Style Exhibition at the Museum of Modern Art. He toured Europe in order to study the works of architects Walter Gropius, Le Corbusier and Mies van der Rohe. By age 80, he had designed the AT&T Building, Pennzoil Place, the Crystal Cathedral, the Lipstick Building in New York City, Transco Tower in Houston and the Pittsburgh Plate Glass company's headquarters. He also designed The Glass House in New Canaan, Connecticut, one of the most famous residences of the 20th century — a structure of floor-to-ceiling glass, steel piers and cylindrical volumes of bricks. It was, he said, "a work of art first and a house second."

Johnson's entry into architecture was also preceded by an aborted political career. His leanings were right wing; fascism fascinated him, especially the national socialism of pre-World War II Nazi Germany. An early defender of Hitler, Johnson praised Nazi rhetoric and style, especially the "look" of blond German boys marching in black boots and smart uniforms. In America, he affiliated himself with the Rev. Coughlin, an anti-Semitic radio personality and Nazi sympathizer. Johnson also helped to form the National Socialists, an American group comprised of former Ku Klux Klan members and other right-wing radicals.

His involvement in all of this came to haunt him once he saw the error of his ways and devoted himself to architecture. For years, the FBI placed him under surveillance and kept ordering him to Washington for questioning. The adverse attention did little to mute his growing fame, however. As Abby Aldrich, one of the founders of the Museum of Modern Art, stated, "Every young man should be allowed to make one large mistake."

Martin Heideggar, Paul de Man and T.S. Eliot were also charged with anti-Semitic behavior during the war, though they did not live to suffer the shame of their mistakes. Franz Schulze, Johnson's biographer, writes that Johnson "felt very ashamed by his early foolishness."

His genius notwithstanding, Johnson could not pass the New York state architecture exam. Because he did not test well, he was obligated to complete a humiliating cram course with younger, far less talented architects at a point in his career where he was able to define Walter Gropius "the Warren B. Harding of architecture," and to publicly intimate that Frank Lloyd Wright was truly great despite a disagreeable personality. Johnson himself was often imperious and a snob, though this in no way prevented him from associating with rough-trade types, nor from having, as he said, "three Mrs. Johnson's in his life," including a handsome Harlem musician who dumped him because Johnson wasn't spending enough time with him. Another love, Jon Stroup, was a lean blond Nordic fellow who lived with Johnson for five years in an open relationship that allowed the architect room to cruise for "the occasional other."

One of Johnson's favorite quotes is from Heraclitus: "Everything flows and nothing abides; everything gives way and nothing stays fixed."

RAINER WERNER FASSBINDER

Toward the end of his life, filmmaker Rainer Werner Fassbinder's goal was to outdo Steven Spielberg's commercial success.

Fassbinder desired this despite the fact that he'd already been credited with restoring German cinema to its pre-Nazi eminence. His dream was cut short by a severe addiction to booze, uppers, downers, LSD and cocaine—all of which conspired to kill him by age 37. In that short time, he managed to write and direct 43 films, 37 screenplays, 15 plays and countless radio scripts. The chain-smoking, overweight director was also a notable stage and screen actor.

"I am not handsome," he told interviewer Boze Hadleigh in 1982. "I indulge in everything...but the superficial power of a filmmaker is an aphrodisiac to many handsome but powerless young men."

Born in 1945, Fassbinder's parents divorced when he was a child. His mother's new husband hated him, forcing the boy to live with his biological father, a slum landlord who forced Rainer to walk the streets and collect the rent. As a young film buff, Fassbinder was rejected by the uppity Berlin Film Institute, an event that soured his views on higher education but which made him regret his lack of a classical education. Even so, he became a fast and furious filmmaker who often joked that making films did not make him suffer.

"If it made me suffer, I would not do much of it," he told Hadleigh. "My work is not cynical. Life is pessimistic in the end, because we die, and it is pessimistic in between, because of corruption in our daily lives. The Hollywood-style critics who like your happy endings would think I'm cynical, but in Europe, in Germany, few mention this."

In 1981, the Berlin Senate agreed to co-finance the film *Querelle* when Fassbinder signed on as director. Having an august political body endorse a major homoerotic opus may seem strange to Americans, but not so to Fassbinder.

"The German people were always liberated about sex," he told Hadleigh. "Homosexuality is not taboo in Germany because it is seen inside the spectrum of sexuality. In America, you have the other problem; they sometimes *tolerate* homosexuals, if they are straight-looking pro-establishment — but they never tolerate *homosexuality*."

Querelle, unlike another German film, *Taxi Zum Klo*, was not a success in the United States. *The Advocate* wrote: "In America, *Querelle* opened and closed quicker than a gay bar in Jerry Falwell's neighborhood." Fassbinder maintained that while all his films did not have a gay subject, they did have the point of view of one gay man.

Fassbinder hated Hollywood-style homosexuals "who acted like they're not homosexual because they don't want to be associated with that. So they become the oppressor."

He told Hadleigh he viewed critics as eunuchs because all they do is watch and criticize because they lack the equipment to *do*.

Vastly overweight, the famed director was a sloppy eater who often got food particles in his mustache, liked to listen to rock 'n' roll and classical music on the radio, and loved to wear black construction boots. At the time of his death, he had a burnt cigarette hanging from his lips and notes for a new film project propped beneath his head. He died four years after his companion, Armin Meier, hanged himself because he believed Fassbinder wasn't paying enough attention to him. Another lover, Hedi ben Salim, also killed himself.

"He could not believe that people could love him," wrote Swiss director Daniel Schmid. "All his life, Rainer thought he was ugly.... The basis for his new friendships was always: You are a pig and I am a pig."

HERMAN MELVILLE

Herman Melville was born in 1819 in New York City. By the time he was 12, his merchant father was dead after being declared insane. At age 15 the future writer was forced to work to support his family. Melville worked as a bank clerk, a teacher and a farm laborer before sailing on a merchant ship to Liverpool. Other sea voyages followed, including a whaling trip from which he jumped ship and lived among the Typee cannibals in the Marquesas.

Melville's experiences in the South Seas provided material for *Typee* (1846), his first book. Novels like *Omoo* (1847), *Mardi* (1849) and *Redburn* (1849), were followed by *White-Jacket* in 1850. These stories dealing with life on the sea not only won Melville popular acclaim, but sparked controversy because they sympathized with pagan societies and questioned western attitudes.

In 1850, Melville and his wife moved to Pittsfield, Massachusetts where they became neighbors and friends of Sophia and Nathaniel Hawthorne. Hawthorne, who was older than Melville, became Melville's mentor and intimate friend.

The relationship had definite erotic overtones. In an anonymous review of one of Hawthorne's books,

Melville wrote: "...I feel that Hawthorne has dropped germanous seeds into my soul. He expands and deepens down, the more I contemplate him; and further and further, shoots his strong New England roots into the hot soil in my southern soul." Under Hawthorne's influence, Melville acquainted himself with a wide range of writers and philosophers. Inspired by his reading, Melville entered into his most ambitious phase.

In 1851, he published *Moby Dick*, a classic work containing many passages about male-male intimacy. The novel's hero, Ishmael, shares his makeshift bed in an inn with an island harpooner. "I tried to move his arm," the hero says, "unlock his bridegroom clasp — yet, sleeping as he was, he still hugged me tightly, as though naught but death should part us twain." In *White-Jacket*, Melville made numerous references to shipboard homosexuality, but in *Pierre or The Ambiguities* (1852), he writes of Pierre's attachment to his cousin, Glen, as something which "transcends the bounds of mere boyishness...it revels in the empyrean of a love which only comes short, by one degree, of the sweetest sentiment entertained between the sexes."

Melville dedicated *Moby Dick* to Hawthorne. Considered by many to be the greatest work of American literature, the book was not well received in 1851. The book's publication marked Melville's fall from popularity into relative obscurity; *Pierre*, a novel of childhood, was scarcely read at all in the 19th century.

At odds with his reading public and separated from Hawthorne (the two had a falling out and Hawthorne also moved to Concord), Melville turned to shorter fiction. At age 40 he wrote only poetry and in 1876 he published "Clarel," a long poem based on a visit to the Holy Land. In "Clarel," Melville does not equate homosexuality with the sin of Sodom and Gomorrah, but says that the biblical cities of the plain were guilty of "Things hard to prove/decorum's wile/Malice indiscreet/judicious guile/Crimes of the spirit."

Melville's various travel journals were published from 1935 to 1955; his collected letters in 1960.

His unfinished tale, *Billy Budd*, did not appear until 1924. *Billy Budd* historian Jonathan Ned Katz writes: "...may be read as a story of love between men—a love blighted and love affirmed. It was in thus affirming the goodness of male-male love that Melville brought his own life's work to a close."

Melville died in 1881.

SAHAYKWISA

According to Walter L. Williams, an ethnohistorian at the University of Southern California, in most Native American cultures an individual's inclinations are seen as due to the influence of spirits. Any outright condemnation of a hwame (an Indian girl who threw away her dolls and aspired to learn masculine skills) or the berdache (a boy who wishes to acquire feminine skills) was seen as a dangerous intrusion into the supernatural. A positive aspect of this belief was that in many tribes, gender roles for women did not restrict their choice of sexual partners. The Mohaves, for instance, expected a hwame girl to marry a woman.

The hwame/berdache Indian was considered by the tribe to possess mystical and healing powers. "Women," writes Native American scholar Paula Gunn Allen, "were perceived to be possessed of a singular power, most vital during menstruation—so powerful that other 'medicines' may be cancelled by the very presence of that power." Women involved with women did not see themselves as a distinct category of woman. For instance, a woman could take a wife, then, when that relationship ended, marry a man and not experience any sort of stigma—gender identity, rather than sexual identity, being the crucial component for the Mohave culture.

Among the stories of the Mohaves, one of the most tragic is that of Sahaykwisa (c. 1860). As a girl, Sahaykwisa may not have thrown away her dolls, but it became evident early on that she was hwame. As with all young hwames, she was initiated in a ritual authorizing her to assume the clothing and engage in the activities of the male sex.

Sahaykwisa, however, retained her normal female dress for the most part. It was said that she had large breasts and that she had occasional sex with white men for money—money she'd spend on her wives or women she wanted to attract. She was a skilled hunter (a man's occupation) and farmer. Considered a shaman, her healing activities were said to cure venereal diseases. Mohaves believed that anyone capable of curing venereal disease was lucky in love, and Sahaykwisa was no exception.

Her first wife was so beautiful men would point at her and say: "A hwame has no penis—she only pokes you with a finger!" Many men tried to lure Sahaykwisa's wife away, and one of them actually succeeded, although the woman returned to Sahaykwisa a little while later. In Mohave marriages, even heterosexual marriages were subject to abrupt endings.

Though the Mohaves accepted hwame marriages, teasing was part of their culture. Sahaykwisa was teased unmercifully. She was called "split vulvae," referring to how the hwame would spread the genitals during sex. Sahaykwisa's wife was taunted so much she left again, this time permanently. When Sahaykwisa courted another woman, the teasing ended this marriage too, causing Sahaykwisa to paint her face black. Undaunted, she propositioned a married woman. The woman spit at her and said: "You think you have a penis!" Sahay-kwisa, unshaken, said: "Yes, I can shoot game for you!" Mohaves believed that if a woman insults her suitor it was an omen of marriage, so Sahaykwisa then offered to grind corn for the woman (a marriage proposal). On the third visit, the woman left with Sahaykwisa.

Unfortunately, the woman's husband ambushed Sahaykwisa one day and raped her. The effect of this on Sahaykwisa was that she stopped courting women. She later became an alcoholic and developed an unhealthy craving for men.

She was thrown into the Colorado River because it was thought that she had bewitched the husband of her third wife. But Sahaykwisa longed for the companion-ship of those she bewitched and was actually looking for a chance to be killed. As Williams writes, "She wanted to join her retinue of ghosts forever."

GEORGE SAND

She was born Aurore Dupin de Francueil—a devout Catholic girl whose education at a French convent school once inspired her to become a nun. She eventually married a law student named Casimir Dudevant, but his abuse ended the marriage, about which Aurore commented to her brother, "Men are not sufficiently aware that their pleasure is a woman's martyrdom."

Taking an apartment in Paris in the 1830s, she wrote a novel, *Rose and Blanche*, with her lover, writer Jules Sandeau under the pen name Jules Sand. Her first novel, *Indiana*, received critical praise from Balzac. She became George Sand when her publisher, searching for a suitable first name, discovered it was St. George's Day.

Her adoption of a male pen name helped reviewers to see *Indiana* in a non-prejudicial light; Sand, quite rightly, congratulated herself on having preempted anti-feminine prejudice. In Paris, she wore men's attire because her long gowns got muddy in the streets and her hats lost their shape in the rain. Men's clothes were more practical: it was easier to go to the theatre in boots, trousers and a waistcoat and sit in the cheap theatre pit (the men's section) instead of the overpriced boxes where the (expensively dressed) ladies were expected to sit.

Additional novels flowed from her pen (one hundred works by the time she was forty-five). She inherited Casimir's estate after a bitter dispute, so was able to live there with her daughter and son. Her string of lovers never abated (she had fourteen in her lifetime). In some Sand biographies, there's an attempt to downplay her love affair with the famous French actress, Marie Dorval. But in 1885, the writer Houssaye wrote, "At the time Sappho loved again in Paris…. An eloquent woman flung her arms round a great actress who had given her life a passion…." Sand herself described Dorval as "so charming as to make prettiness superfluous. Her face was more than a face, it was a soul." The relationship caused a fair amount of gossip but it did not prevent Sand from writing plays for Dorval in which both their names appeared on advertisements, causing further speculation. Sand's ex-husband used her friendship with Dorval to further discredit her in the eyes of the public. Sand, always faithful to the dictates of her heart, remained undaunted.

Sand advocated a peculiar brand of socialism based on "Christian humanitarianism," and many of her novels had socialist messages. Not orthodox in a religious sense (she never went to mass), she nevertheless found favor with a philosopher named Leroux whose philosophy she adopted in many mystical novels. Her belief in the full equality of women in marriage caused her to criticize the institution as it was promulgated in 19th century France. Women's rights organizations, for instance, attempted to draft her to head a movement supporting women's right to vote, but Sand withdrew, claiming that political rights could not be gained until personal equality rights in marriage became the norm.

Sand could write anywhere, anytime, and was faithful to her regime of writing eight hours a night, usually when her children were asleep and after a day of walking in the woods (sometimes with Frederic Chopin, her most famous lover, who'd follow her on a donkey). Despite her genius, she had problems with spelling, syntax and grammar and needed good editors to go over her manuscripts. She found it difficult to engage in small talk and so retreated into herself at large gatherings, astonishing people like Charles Dickens who expected something else entirely.

This fiercely independent and passionate woman caused Flaubert to write, "At her funeral I cried like an ass."

HENRY GERBER
Starting a Movement Before Its Time

Born in 1892, Henry Gerber had no idea he was gay until after his 21st birthday. The year 1914 found him as a United States Army combat soldier in Europe where he became acquainted with the early German homosexual emancipation movement. Inspired by what he saw, on his return to the United States in 1924, he collaborated with six other men to establish the Society for Human Rights. The society was chartered by the state of Illinois until local authorities arrested Gerber and his associates. As a result of the crackdown, Gerber lost his job and his savings.

Disillusioned but not defeated, Gerber moved to New York City in 1928 where he wrote for a number of German gay periodicals. Prophetic writing was not among his major talents: "In America," he wrote in 1928, "the Christian religion is losing ground and the horizon is growing brighter for homosexuals." Gerber worked as a U.S. Army proofreader and used Army supplies and equipment to publish "Contacts," his newsletter for gay pen pals. The paper also served to coordinate introductions between gay men. Gerber's pilfering of Army supplies went undetected, though the newsletter eventually folded.

In 1932, he published his essay, "In Defense of Homosexuality" in *The Modern Thinker*. His thesis was that it was not the business of government to interfere in the sexual lives of adults as long as the rights of others were not violated.

One of the men who answered Gerber's ad in "Contacts" was Manual Boyfrank, a 39-year-old Californian. Boyfrank and Gerber found they had much in common intellectually, though they were not sexually compatible—Gerber being attracted exclusively to 20ish-year-old men. The two men did begin an intense correspondence, however, which lasted most of their lives. Boyfrank's wish was to begin an organization that would fight discrimination against homosexuals. Jonathan Katz, in the *Gay and Lesbian Almanac*, says that Boyfrank "wanted to use the interest of male homosexuals in romantic contacts as a means of organizing them against their persecution," whereas Gerber "wanted to convince the authorities to repeal anti-homosexual laws." When "Contacts" was resurrected in 1944, Gerber said it was the Society of Human Rights all over again, but with the sex element disguised.

Gerber regretted that most homosexuals were "too scared to give their names, or to join any association trying to help them." He was also unhappy that so many men were only interested in physical contacts and had no desire to help their own cause.

Gerber believed that homosexuality was nature's own birth control. "It is less of a perversion than artificial birth control," he said. "With the [WWII] condom shortage, it is even patriotic to be homosexual." At age 52, he no longer believed "in martyrdom for the sake of others. The individual or the group cannot change the severely slow progress of evolution, especially when religion and politics pull in the opposite direction," he wrote.

Gerber remarked that he had "no confidence in the 'Dorian' crowd" because when the going got rough, "homosexuals skipped out." In 1946, an aging Gerber found time to translate into English portions of Magnus Hirschfeld's *Homosexuality in Man and Woman.*

Gerber died in 1969, just after the Stonewall uprising in New York City.

SYLVIA BEACH

Paris in the 1920s was a place in time unlike any other. Former medical school student Gertrude Stein left Baltimore to become a resident. Writers F. Scott Fitzgerald, Sherwood Anderson, Ernest Hemingway, Henry Miller, Djuna Barnes, Anais Nin and lesbian socialite Natalie Barney soon followed.

Largely responsible for this renaissance was 30-year old Sylvia Beach, a lanky American-born book lover with bobbed hair. From her earliest years, this only daughter of a liberal Presbyterian minister wanted to open a bookshop in New York or London. In 1917, she met Adrienne Monnier, who was then the proprietor of The Book Lovers' Home, the first lending library in Paris. After becoming lovers, Beach and Monnier, fueled by a love of books and literature, pooled their resources to realize Beach's dream. After considerable delay, Shakespeare & Company, a bookstore specializing in American books, was born.

Beach inherited her father's missionary zeal, but instead of converting infidels, she wanted to bring the works of American authors to the French reading public. Her rejection of worldly goods and her total devotion to art was monastic in the extreme. Her humble apartment above the shop contained no kitchen or bath, and she continued to use a bicycle when everyone else was driving cars.

Totally self-educated ("I never went to school and wouldn't have learned anything if I had," she once boasted), Beach taught herself French, Italian and Spanish and read voraciously until her death.

In 1920 she met James Joyce. At this time excerpts from Joyce's *Ulysses* had been published in magazines, but not in book form. Beach knew Joyce was a genius and so stocked her store with copies of *Portrait of the Artist as a Young Man*. She also introduced Joyce to critics and talked up his work whenever she could. Her most important role, however, would be as Joyce's publisher — *Ulysses* being her sole publishing venture. Beach allowed Joyce the freedom to correct proofs in his own handwriting (often there were more corrections than copy). On several occasions, the publication of the book was delayed because of Joyce's revisions. Complicating the situation were mounting legal sanctions against the work (the serialization in the United States, by lesbian editor Margaret Anderson, had to be stopped because of U.S. obscenity charges). For ten years, *Ulysses* was smuggled out of Shakespeare & Company to all parts of the world. Eleven editions of the book were necessary before it was picked up and reissued by Random House.

Beach's publishing endeavor, while assuring her a spot in literary history, did not make her rich. If anything, publication and mailing expenses set her back, and the royalties from the book were not very good. Beach's publication of *Ulysses* also gave other writers the wrong idea: artists like D.H. Lawrence, Henry Miller, Frank Harris and others all had erotic works rejected by Beach. Beach thought the writing in *Lady Chatterly's Lover* "overwrought," but the real reason for her rejection was her disinterest in erotica.

During World War II, Beach, still an American citizen, was imprisoned briefly by the Nazis. After the war, friends urged her to reopen the shop, but Beach refused, realizing an era had come to an end. Monnier's tragic suicide in 1955 after a lengthy illness propelled Beach to write her autobiography. She was awarded the Legion d'Honneur in 1937 and an honorary doctorate from the University of Buffalo in 1961. This extraordinary missionary for American literature died of a heart attack in 1963.

MINOR WHITE

Minor White, one of the most important American photographers of the post-World War II era, was born in 1908 and studied botany at the University of Minnesota before teaching himself photography.

Using his grandfather's equipment, White went to work for the Works Progress Administration, a Depression-era agency where he did historical documentation. By the time he was awarded the Bronze Star in 1945, he had already made a name for himself as a photographer in San Francisco and Portland, Oregon.

After WWII, White visited the New York studio of Alfred Stieglitz in an attempt to regain his artistic direction. Stieglitz asked him, "Have you been in love?" When White said yes, Stieglitz told him, "Then you can photograph."

Influenced by Ansel Adams, Edward Steichan and Edward Weston, most of White's austere studies of rock formations, seascapes and man-made structures are rich in phallic symbolism. In *Mirrors, Messages Manifestations*, a survey of his works published in his lifetime, White combined photographs with poetry he wrote while stationed in the Philippines. In 1947, his 50-print, 50-verse exhibition, *Amputations*, was rejected at San

Francisco's Palace of the Legion of Honor because of the length and sloppiness of his writing style. While critics were sympathetic to White's photographic work, his writing was seen as intellectually vague and overly mystical.

White's World War II photographs show the intimacy of men in combat. While still a soldier, he wrote a friend: "There is much of unalloyed lust among men without women, that fine bodies in close proximity and lads with limbs as smooth as a woman's does noting to lessen..."

His picture sequence, *Song Without Words,* includes portraits with atmospheric seascapes. One 1949 photograph is a contemporary-looking portrait of two men embracing. The men sport crew cuts, white shirts and black ties. Their overt affection is White's homage to "the love that dare not speak its name," despite the fact that most of White's male nudes avert their faces in what Allen Ellenzweig, author of *The Homoerotic Photograph,* calls "a chilling reminder of the public state of homosexuality from the late 1940's until the Stonewall Rebellion."

"Homoerotic," wrote C.J. Jung, "is always associated with an etiology that involves a religious crisis or a religious quest; homosexual refers merely to a matter of practice in sexual behavior." Ellenzweig says that to understand White's homoeroticism it is necessary to understand the intense religious character of his quest. "It was through his personal search for spiritual enlightenment," he writes, "that his photography ultimately achieved its potent metaphysical quality."

In the '50s and '60s, White taught at the Massachusetts Institute of Technology and worked as an editor. In his personal life, his spiritual goals were oftentimes at odds with feelings of carnal lust. A convert to Catholicism, White also studied Zen Buddhism and adopted Gurdjieff's philosophy. His frail body, a friend once said, was "topped by long white hair, and a monkish posture often in Zen repose."

William La Rue (whom White photographed) was his traveling companion and workshop assistant for a number of years. White also took in many of his young male students as boarders. If there was a homoerotic aspect to these living arrangements, it had to do with sexual tension, not sexual activity. A friend, James Baker Hall, remarked: "He found great pleasure in simply being with men, especially young men, in working with them and teaching them and photographing them."

✦

ROBERT MAPPLETHORPE
The Artist Jesse Helms Loved to Hate

"I went into photography because it seemed like the perfect vehicle for commenting on the madness of today's existence."
—Robert Mapplethorpe

Robert Michael Mapplethorpe was one of four children born to Harry and Joan Mapplethorpe on November 4, 1946, in Queens, New York. He was his mother's favorite child. Harry Mapplethorpe, a "straight shooter" who had a talent for fixing broken vacuum cleaners, forced Robert to play baseball, despite the fact that his son was gangly and uncoordinated. Robert's interests were home jewelry-making kits, his own Picasso-inspired Madonna sketches, and jumping on Pogo Sticks. Before he was 10, the future S&M photographer was named the Pogo-Stick Champion of 259th Street.

As a teenager, Mapplethorpe worked at the Belgian Pavillion at the 1964 World's Fair. He also made trips to 42nd Street, where he stole gay porn from a blind newsstand proprietor. He enrolled in the famed Pratt Institute, where he came to hate his photography courses and where he joined the ROTC and the elite Pershing

Rifle Corps, a clique of gung-ho jocks. In the '60s, he traded the ROTC for long hair and hippie garb, a move that further alienated him from his father.

The climax of Mapplethorpe's student years occurred when he "killed" his beloved pet monkey by forgetting to feed him. In a Dahmeresque ritual, he then boiled the head and made a work of art out of the monkey's skull.

Mapplethorpe met rocker/poet Patti Smith when Smith wandered into his apartment by mistake. Within a year, they'd shared a series of dingy apartments and lofts. Mapplethorpe did not yet know what kind of artist he was, but Smith was hung up on [French] poets Arthur Rimbaud and Paul Verlaine, disrobing in public, and taking every drug she could lay her hands on. She'd often run through the streets screaming that she had seen God and that she knew the purpose of life.

His coming out was slow and painful. Part of the problem was his fear of offending Jehovah's Witness-born Patti Smith who, despite her love of the avant-garde, used words like 'faggot' and who thought homosexuality unnatural. Although Patricia Morrisroe, in her 1995 biography *Mapplethorpe*, alleges that Mapplethorpe and Smith were lovers, author Felice Picano, who dismisses the biography as "totally deluded" begs to disagree: "I knew him [Mapplethorpe] well. It is doubtful he ever slept with any woman, including La Smith."

Picano, who art directed many books published by Gay Presses in his native New York in the 1970s, who in that capacity also worked with Mapplethorpe, utilizing one of his photos for the cover of an early Seahorse Press edition, goes on to say: "Not only wasn't Robert in *any way* interested in women sexually, as Morrisroe tried to persuade readers—we used to kid him mercilessly about Lisa Lyons, the woman bodybuilder he photographed so often...*because*, Robert said, she looked like a guy—"

Mapplethorpe's parents assumed he was straight, even after the controversy surrounding *The Perfect Moment* exhibition in 1989. Robert was a regular at bars like the Mineshaft and Keller's, where he'd take home as many as six or seven men a day. "I am a demon of sex," he was fond of saying. His advice to gay men was: "When you make love to someone, always make room for Satan."

The Perfect Moment, opened at the Institute of Contemporary Art in Philadelphia on December 9, 1988. The exhibit, which included photographs of men engaged in sadomasochistic activities, ran for over a month and closed without ruffling feathers. Having attended the opening, I remember long lines outside the ICA. The crowd was subdued, and if anyone was shocked by the X-rated photographs in a separate display case, they kept their feelings to themselves. People knew what they were in for, and *American Gothic* types, or *Scarlet Letter* Puritans simply stayed away.

In 1989, *The Perfect Moment* attracted national attention when Corcoran Gallery of Art director, Christina Orr-Cahall, caving in to threats by North Carolina Republican Senator Jesse Helms to withhold government funds for art works depicting sadomasochism and homosexuality, cancelled the exhibition. Orr-Cahill's actions came after *The Perfect Moment* had enjoyed a peaceful run in Chicago. Later, Orr-Cahill would come to regret her actions and said in a statement: "Our course in the future will be to support art, artists and freedom of artistic expression."

Mapplethorpe called his little studio at 24 Bond Street his "art factory" (after Warhol), where he managed to employ a homophobic but talented printer named Tom Baril. Thanks to a $500,000 gift from millionaire Sam Wagstaff, who became Mapplethorpe's financial patron, he was able to buy the Bond Street studio. Through Wagstaff, Mapplethorpe was able to meet gallery owners and make valuable connections. Many in the New York art world maintain that without Wagstaff's help, Mapplethorpe's work would have gone unnoticed.

"Wagstaff resembled Gary Cooper, and like the actor, projected an idealized version of American manhood; he was over six feet tall, with sandy-colored hair, large gray-blue eyes, sensuous lips, a strong nose and jaw, and dimpled cheeks," Patricia Morrisroe wrote in her (aforementioned) biography. "Sam was remarkable looking," said art dealer Klaud Kertess. "I watched him swim once and I never saw such grace. You could not look at him without desire."

"Mapplethorpe is so dirty," Andy Warhol once said. "His feet stink. He has no money." Mapplethorpe also had a tendency to use people, especially when he'd bring home tricks to photograph and have sex with. He nearly always ordered them out of the studio the following morning. According to Morrisroe, Mapplethorpe's superficial charisma wore off as one got to know him. When he latched onto black men as objects of desire (and art), he delighted in calling them "niggers" because he said that the word gave them hard-ons. Milton Moore ("Man in Polyester Suit," 1980), Robert's black lover of three years, said of their relationship: "I think he saw me like a monkey in a zoo."

Mapplethorpe died from HIV-AIDS complications in 1989. At his funeral Mass, the priest reminded the mourners that there is a dark side to the human soul that is filled with conflict and torment. "It is a side of the human soul that few people are brave enough to explore," Morrisroe recorded the priest as saying.

PAUL CADMUS

In the 1930s, Paul Cadmus' paintings generated as much controversy as Robert Mapplethorpe's photographs did in the 1980s.

With provocative titles such as *YMCA Locker Room*, *Shore Leave*, *The Seven Deadly Sins* and *Sailors and Floosies*, Cadmus' egg-yolk tempera compositions caused critic Lewis Mumford of 'The New Yorker' to say that, "one comes pretty close to hating the artist himself for giving one such an unpalatable mouthful."

Born in 1904 in New York City, Cadmus published his first sketch in 'The New York Herald-Tribune' when he was 10, and entered the National Academy of Design five years later. In 1927, he had his first solo show at a gallery in New Hope. Later, he traveled to Europe, where he befriended novelist E. M. Forester.

His life as an obscure painter in Greenwich Village ended when his painting, *The Fleet's In!* was removed from the first exhibition of New Deal art at the Corcoran Gallery in Washington, D.C. Other artists used their government-sponsored paintings to please patrons, but not Cadmus, who angered the philistines with what Philip Eliasoph, author of *Paul Cadmus, Yesterday and Today*, called "his explicit sexual depiction of anxious sailors and whores carousing in Riverside Park."

At the time, Navy officials insisted that Cadmus' painting be destroyed. Cadmus told Navy officials that his painting represented what he'd witnessed in the park, namely loose women and gay men offering themselves to drunken, war-weary sailors.

Other run-ins with the Navy and government officials followed. His 1940 painting, *Sailors and Floosies*, was banned from an exhibition in San Francisco. He also was ordered to "re-touch" his Treasury Department-commissioned mural of Pocahontas and John Smith because it was "too risqué."

Life, Esquire, and *Newsweek* all reported on Cadmus, "the enfant terrible" of the 1930s who boasted in interviews and in personal letters that his mission was "to explore bankrupt bourgeois values." During this period, he describes himself as being "a little pink" because of his alliance with leftist organizations.

Categorized by critics as a "story-telling, representational artist," Eliasoph adds that Cadmus' work can be seen as a series of "painted novels." Eliasoph wrote: "Homosexuality permeates his imagery.... Sometimes there are contradictions in these paintings, for carnal lust is juxtaposed with the most intense idealism.... No other American artist has been so sincere and delicate, so realistic and romantic, so erotic and yet not exploitive about homosexuality."

Today, Cadmus' work has slipped from view, and is seldom mentioned in the world of art.

Before his death several years ago, Cadmus lived in rural Connecticut, "off a dirt road," according to Eliasoph. In a letter, quoted by Eliasoph, Cadmus maintained that he doesn't love humanity "in the theatrical, papal way, nor in the Mother Teresa way." Although he could not, he said, "love the poor, deformed, ugly and mean," he did say that he hated what made them that way.

ANNA FREUD

Anna Freud (1895-1982) was born in Vienna. As the youngest of six children, she often described her childhood as "naughty" and "wild." Anna never completed college and it is said that she lamented her lack of a classical education all her life.

Anna, the founder of child psychiatry, became a psychoanalyst after spending five years teaching elementary school. She learned analysis from her father, who psychoanalyzed her before parent-child analysis sessions were ruled "dangerous." Anna's first sessions were conducted with the children of Dorothy Burlington, her companion for 25 years. Burlington was from a wealthy family and had four children from a previous marriage. Anna helped raise two of those children, dubbing herself the children's "psychological mother."

Despite Sigmund Freud's extensive work in the area of sexuality and the unconscious (Freud maintained that everyone is bisexual), Anna was guilt-ridden when it came to issues like masturbation and lesbianism. Her first paper was called "Beating Fantasies and Daydreams", which was concerned with the methods people used to try and stop masturbating. Regarding Anna's lesbianism, author Dell Richards comments: "The (Freud/Burlington) relationship fit the continuum of romantic friend-lesbian relationships that began centuries earlier and runs through the personal denial of the mid-20th century up to the political awakening of the post-Stonewall era.... The general public didn't think anything of it, however, until people like Anna's father began theorizing about women's sexuality and exposed the deceptive innocence of the romantic relationships."

Dorothy and Anna ran a series of training/analysis schools for children during their lifelong relationship. Because Dorothy had made a commitment to care for her elderly parents, the two women were unable to live together until they were in their fifties, although they'd bought a house in Ireland where they could vacation together.

During WWII, the Nazis invaded Sigmund Freud's house in Vienna, stealing money and destroying many artifacts. When the Freud family decided to leave the city, they were made to wait three months before the move was approved. This was a painful time during which the family fully expected to be killed or sent to a concentration camp. Indeed, Anna herself *was* taken prisoner, but missed being sent to a camp by pretending to be a political, rather than an ethnic prisoner. She was eventually released as a result of her quick thinking.

After her father's death from cancer (the disease caused Freud to have half his jawbone and cheek removed), Anna and Dorothy published *Young Children in Wartime* and *Infants Without Families*. In 1941, they founded the Hampstead Child Therapy Clinic.

Anna and Dorothy's relationship suffered a temporary collapse when Dorothy left for the United States and became involved with a man. She wrote Anna of her infatuation and confusion, but realized her mistake when she didn't hear back from Anna. Though Anna's silence was due to a postal problem, Dorothy imagined that she had so devastated Anna that she was incapable of responding. Dorothy, thinking that she had ruined her life as well as any future she might have had with Anna, returned home, and the two resumed their relationship on even more intimate terms until Dorothy's death in 1979.

After her companion's death, Anna sold the house in Ireland because she didn't want to be reminded of happier times. "Her latter years were filled with concerns about the clinic she and Dorothy had founded," Richard writes. "A bequest from actress Marilyn Monroe, who had been analyzed by a friend of Anna's, solved many of her financial worries."

JOHN RECHY

Contemporary gay male fiction concentrates on similar themes: AIDS, coming out or coming of age, middle-class men falling in love. One writer who has ignored these templates is John Rechy.

In *Gay Sunshine*, an anthology published in the 1970s, Rechy writes about what he calls, "the real hero of the gay world — the promiscuous homosexual."

Another writer who laments the current state of gay literature is Felice Picano. In 1993, Picano told *Torso* magazine, "Often the only 'real gay literature' are books by gays which do everything they can to efface the fact that the authors and characters are gays. They're 'Books Without Dicks' because the gay characters in them give no proof whatsoever by speech or action that they have genitalia and actually use it. The worst offenders in this are the short-story collections of David Leavitt and Michael Cunningham's first novel."

Gay critics and straight reviewers, Picano insists, take these books as examples of what gays should write.

"They do this openly — by saying they are great and other gay books are not — and covertly — by reviewing these kinds of books and not others," he said in *Torso*.

But it is Rechy, more than any other gay American writer, who has had the most contempt for bourgeois morality. Born in El Paso, Texas, to a Mexican mother and a Scottish father, Rechy wound up in New York after college and a stint in the U.S. Army. His first novel, *City of Night*, (1963) began as a series of letters to a friend. Rechy sent "the letters" to *Evergreen* magazine and *New Directions* and received two acceptance letters.

Now considered a classic, *City of Night* is a hustler/narrator's odyssey through the American gay world in the '60s. In an interview with *Gay Sunshine's* Winston Leyland, Rechy said he had a ferocious need to hustle.

"There's no rush in my life like it," he said. "I am what is called promiscuous, and I love having contacts with one person after another."

Conservative homosexuals were not happy with Rechy's books. Rechy called conservative homosexuals "odious, like blacks who wanted to straighten their hair…. They want to be straighter than straight and just show the best part of our lives."

"I feel an element of despair is very real in gay life," he said. "It's not an indictment of the gay world to say that it's a very depressing, lonely world in many aspects. It is so with any other pressured minority. For example, it's fine to be black, but the situations that surround being black certainly do not make it a totally joyous experience."

Rechy's next three books, *Numbers* (1967), *This Day's Death* (1969) and *The Vampires* (1971), were criticized for their bleak, despondent picture of gay life.

"But I must tell what I experience," he insisted in *Gay Sunshine*.

After *City of Night* was published, Rechy moved back to El Paso, and then to Los Angeles a year later, where he found himself "out of control and courting sexual encounters." This experience formed the basis of *The Sexual Outlaw*, a non-fiction book.

Rechy, who resides in Hollywood, California, does not hide his hatred of homosexuals who have loathsome attitudes toward themselves, and his mistrust of the police is legendary.

"I can't understand how cops can move into an area and do whatever the fuck they want and not one gay person asks, 'What right do you have to do what you are doing?'"

VITA SACKVILLE-WEST

In the 1950s, she had a syndicated gardening column in several English newspapers. The lilies, tulips, cyclamen and peonies she wrote about sanitized a personal life that would have shocked the English middle class. [English royalty has a centuries-old tradition of following its own moral code: Kings were expected to have mistresses; members of the royal family were permitted to break social taboos that would have landed ordinary mortals in jail. Prince Charles' former sexual philandering, despite the manic reactions of the media, has the blessing of History.]

Vita Sackville-West was born at Knole, England in 1892. In 1913 she married Harold Nicholson, a gay diplomat and later a House of Parliament member. Seemingly heterosexual at the time of their marriage, both came out late in life, but rather than divorce they decided to make the most of their commonality and shared interests. "After a few difficult years trying to integrate a love life into their marriage, they realized they could be secret gay allies in a hostile, heterosexual world," writes Dell Richards. Vita had the habit of transforming her lovers into lifelong friends. Moody and unpredictable, she'd end relationships quickly and without warning. The physical aspect of her relationship with novelist Virginia Woolf, for instance, was short but their friendship endured for life [Woolf later used Vita as the model for her novel, *Orlando*]. About Virginia, Vita wrote: "I am scared to death of arousing physical feelings in her because of the madness. I don't know what effect it would have, you see; it is a fire with which I have no wish to play...I have gone to bed with her twice, but that's all."

Vita kept her marriage to Harold intact because she wished to maintain her social standing. Satisfied with the arrangement, Harold agreed to let her come and go as she wished. Often she'd leave for months at a time. Only one woman — Violet Trefusis — threatened the stability of her marriage. [Her memoir about her affairs with Violet was published privately in 1923.]

Vita's first book of poetry, *Harth and Apples*, was published in 1917. She was a best selling novelist in her day, though critics say she had a tendency to copy Virginia Woolf's style.

"Not much to my severer taste — florid, moustached, parakeet-coloured, with all the supple ease of the aristocracy, but not the wit of the artist...Vita finds me incredibly dowdy — there is some voluptuousness about her; the grapes are ripe; and not reflective. In brain and insight she is not as highly organized as I am," was Woolf's first impression of Vita. In 1935, Virginia realized that her passionate friendship with Vita was over. There'd been no quarrel, no outward sign of coolness, no bitterness.

Vita's popularity as a poet waned once T.S. Eliot began publishing his verse. Her sweeping verses on the glories of nature found ready audiences in middlebrow women's magazines but otherwise went unnoticed. Her newspaper gardening column won her popular acclaim in England; even the Queen Mother saw her as an expert on every facet of gardening. Her collected gardening columns covered ten published volumes in all.

Vita's estate at Sissinghurst was famous through-out England for its beautiful gardens. She spared no expense importing tulip bulbs, exotic roses and large numbers of herbs like herba barona, vervain and wormwoxl. For Vita, buying for the garden came before buying clothes.

Vita Sackville-West died of cancer in 1962 at age 76. A decade after her death, her son, Neigel Nicholson, published *Portrait of a Marriage,* a book about his parents' open, bisexual marriage.

ALICE TOKLAS
More Than Just Brownies

She ended her life in a small, sterile apartment on Paris' rue de la Convention as the nurse who cared for her slammed doors and regulated the flow of visitors. Some years before, she was evicted from her place on the rue Christine that she shared with Gertrude Stein for 25 years.

The eviction was aided in part by the Stein family who were the legal inheritors of art treasures amassed by Gertrude during her lifetime. Drawings and sketches by Cezanne, Juan Gris and Pablo Picasso were sold by the family for six million, while Alice was permitted to sell only occasional pieces when she needed cash.

This odd codicil was engineered by Gertrude herself and to many it seemed like a betrayal of the woman who was Gertrude's handmaiden, typist, cook, lover, companion and literary executor. The Stein family's greed reached pathological proportions when they threatened to take Toklas to court when she sold a print the family had overlooked when they ransacked the rue Christine apartment.

Author James Lord, in his essay on Toklas in his book *Six Exceptional Women*, says that Toklas never let the actions of the Stein family taint her memory of Gertrude. Alice saw to the publication of all of Gertrude's unpublished manuscripts with the same tenacity she showed in acquiescing to all of Gertrude's wishes. Picasso, whose monumental portrait of Stein hung over the rue Christine fireplace, often insisted that Gertrude was really a fascist pig with a weakness for Franco.

"If you want to see how much she really understands about painting, all you have to do is look at the crap she likes now. She says the same things about Hemingway, too. Hemingway was a phony. I always knew that, but Gertrude didn't know it."

About Toklas, Picasso mused: "That little witch: do you know why she wears her hair in bangs? She has a horn."

As guests at rue Christine discovered, "conversations" with Gertrude were monologues that Stein *performed*; not even Alice was permitted to voice a different opinion, lest she risk suffering the wrath of Gertrude. Interesting, then, that Picasso would say, "Gertrude and Alice were really the same person in a way, only different parts."

During World War II when American soldiers visited the pair, Lord says that "Gertrude talked, the soldiers listened and everybody was happy. I wondered about Miss Toklas. She sat quietly by, seldom participating other than to pass the delicious cookies she had made or, when pressed for an opinion, to agree automatically with some pronouncement of Miss Stein's." Lord also states that the striking imbalance between the social statuses of the two women was disconcerting. "Whatever their private relations may have been, in public Alice was the inferior...as I returned regularly to the rue Christine, I had become more and more aware of Miss Stein's monolithic egotism."

Thom Nickels

After Gertrude's death, Alice became a celebrated figure in her own right. Lord says her voice was throaty, lower than Gertrude's, but more melodious. She loved to talk, to eat in restaurants. Often she wore a flat-brimmed black hat festooned with ostrich feathers.

In 1961, Alice returned from a trip to Italy to find the rue Christine apartment stripped of artwork, the Stein family having waited until Alice was away before storing the treasures in a Chase Manhattan Bank vault. They then waited for the old lady to die.

Alice lived in the denuded apartment until 1964 when she was finally forced to move. She spent the last three years of her life in bed. "I'd be fine if it weren't for that dreadful woman," she said of her nurse. "She makes life miserable for me in every way she can." Alice died in March 1967, a few weeks before her 90th birthday. She was buried next to Gertrude in the Cemetery of Pere Lachaise, her name inscribed in the back of the same tombstone.

The Beautiful Teenage Genius Poet
ARTHUR RIMBAUD

From Jim Morrison to Patti Smith, from Henry Miller to Jean Genet, Jean-Nicholas-Arthur Rimbaud has probably influenced more artists than any other writer. "Change your life!" he wrote. "Everything we are taught is false!"

Rimbaud was born October 20, 1854. His mother came from a family of farmers. Frederic Rimbaud, his father, was an infantry captain. Arthur's early years at school were spent at the Institution Rossat in Charleville, where his academic excellence enabled him to skip several grades.

At 13, he was writing letters in Latin hexameters to the imperial prince. At 15, his Latin poem, "Jugurtha," won an important literary prize. His first known French poem, "Les Etrennes des Orphelins," was composed in the same year. At 16 he wrote: "What does it matter to me whether I have a degree? What's the point of a degree? What good is it? They say you can't get a job without a degree. But I don't want a job."

His poetic genius was fully manifest while still a teenager. At 16 he'd already completed 22 poems and sent some of them for publication to *Le Parnasse Contemporain*. He also left his mother's farm and ran away to Paris. Penniless and alone, he was picked up by some soldiers on a train and brutally initiated into sex. The result of this experience, says English writer A.L. Rowse, was a brilliant poem "filled with untranslatable, bitter slang." At the end of this fateful trip, he was imprisoned because he did not have a train ticket. Georges Izambard, his mentor and teacher, secured his release.

He sent a number of his poems to poet Paul Verlaine (age 27), then living in Paris with his wife, Mathilde, who later divorced him. Impressed with Rimbaud's work, Verlaine invited the poet to visit him. He was shocked to discover that the author was a boy who possessed great facial beauty and penetrating eyes. Rouse describes Rimbaud at this time as being "...full of vigor: a passionate sensuality emanating from all his features." Rimbaud enabled Verlaine to write again while the older poet helped Rimbaud to subordinate his eccentricities to the demands of art. Rimbaud wanted his poetry to go beyond Baudelaire's "disordering of the senses." His aim was to transcend ordinary reality and explore the dream life. He also wanted to become a seer and to penetrate the secrets of God.

In 1871, their stormy physical relationship culminated in an exchange of explicit and raunchy erotic poems (published by Gay Sunshine Press in 1979 as "A Lover's Cock"). The pair scandalized polite Paris society when they went to the opera draped in each other's arms. They traveled to London where they quickly became destitute. Verlaine taught French for extra cash. They argued in Brussels, where Verlaine shot Rimbaud in the wrist. He served two years in prison for the assault, the long sentence due partially to the judge's homophobia.

Rimbaud wrote much of his prose poem, "Illuminations," in 1867 while in London. He composed "Une

Saison en Enfer," his most famous work, in 1873 at his mother's farm in Roche.

Rimbaud stopped writing at age 20 and began his life as a vagabond with a trek across Europe. He ended up in Egypt and Aden, where he took an Arab boy as his lover and where he worked as a coffee and gun exporter. A tumor in his right knee caused him to return to France. He died in Marseille at 37 years of age.

Paul Verlaine spent the rest of his life looking for boys who resembled the 16-year-old genius who had so transformed his life.

DR. MARY WALKER
"The Most Distinguished Sexual Invert in the U.S.A."

In a New York Public Library photograph, Dr. Mary Walker resembles a clean-shaven Abraham Lincoln: the jacket, shirt, stiff collar, bow tie and top hat being a style of dress she adopted towards the end of her life. Although this "fashion statement" had definite feminist ideological roots, it didn't win Walker many admirers. Feminists and suffragists, put off by Walker's attire, also distanced themselves from this Oswego, New York-born curmudgeon when she insisted that a female suffrage law was not necessary because the U.S. Constitution already "gave" women the vote.

Dr. Walker began to criticize the restrictive aspects of female clothing when she was a young girl. Later, she was one of the first activist-writers to promote the ideas of the feminist dress reform movement. This occurred around 1850 when Amelia Bloomer introduced the female pants outfit. By then Dr. Walker was already a practicing physician, having graduated from Syracuse Medical College in 1855. At this time she married fellow MD, Albert Miller, although she never took his name and the marriage did not last. Historians agree that sexual incompatibility and Dr. Walker's puritanical views on sex were the probable reasons for the marriage's failure.

In her first book, *Hit*, which she dedicated to her parents and "To the Practical Dress Reformers," she lashed out at women being treated as "dolls" by men, and at women losing their surnames in marriage. She also suggested that married men adopt the term "Misterer," as married women are called "Missis," and she encouraged mothers to teach their sons housekeeping. Dr. Walker was also concerned about the "unequal distribution of capital" as it affected workingwomen.

Her second book, *The Science of Immorality*, published in Philadelphia in 1878, profiled her puritanical feminism, an incongruent oddity considering her radical transvestism and a 1902 medical journal article's reference to her as "the most distinguished sexual invert in the United States."

In *The Science of Immorality*, she commented on an 1861 study by phrenologists Fowler and Wells on masturbation among the young, saying: "Tobacco, intoxicating drinks, pepper, and the heating and dragging of the mother's clothing, all affect the boy in utero so that an effort for relief is made by masturbation.... No one can practice this vice without the sure marks of the same being left in the face.... The effects of this vice are consumption, insanity, softening of the brain and disease of the cuticle." She also condemned heterosexual anal intercourse, "Turkish pederasty" and heterosexual oral sex.

Dr. Walker's thinking was subject to the sexual superstition of the day. "Her book's eccentricities are probably no greater than many other sex and medical manuals of the day, while its underlying, deep-felt concern for women and its angry feminism distinguish it from other works of this genre," Jonathan Katz writes in *Gay American History*. Katz also feels that Dr. Walker's emphasis on procreation would seem to "rule out any conscious sanctioning of Lesbian activity, this being something that Walker probably directed into non-sexual channels."

During the Civil War, Dr. Walker volunteered her services in Union army hospitals. She was captured by the Confederates, released, and then sent to work in Kentucky, where her cantankerous personality won her few friends. For a while she lived with Belva Lockwood in Washington, D.C., where both women worked in the women's suffrage movement. Although she was award-ed the Congressional Medal of Honor for her work during the Civil War, a federal review board declared in 1917 that the medal was undeserved and rescinded the citation. Dr. Walker continued to wear the medal until her death in 1919, when, Katz says, she died "poor and alone."

OSCAR WILDE

Oscar O'Flahertie Wills Wilde was born into a family of writers. His mother, Lady Jane Francesca, wrote nationalistic poems and prose pieces under the pen name Speranza. Her book, *Ancient Legends, Mystic Charms and Superstitions of Ireland*, was published in 1887. Wilde's father, Sir William, was an Irish antiquarian and surgeon who specialized in diseases of the eye and the ear. His primary theme as a writer was archaeological history, and he published one book, *Irish Popular Superstitions*, in 1852. After Sir William's death in 1876, Wilde's mother settled in London, where she began a career as a hostess of a literary salon.

Young Oscar attended Trinity College in Dublin and later won a scholarship to Oxford. At Oxford he turned to poetry, read Walter Pater, and cultivated an aesthetic philosophy known as Art for Art's Sake. Interested in fashion and culture, Wilde wore velvet knee breeches and collected blue china and peacock's feathers. While a student, the future playwright made no secret of his disdain for athleticism.

Wilde won several poetry awards at Oxford, and in 1881 published his first volume of poems. This early work attracted little attention. (An essay on Wilde, published by the School District of Philadelphia for the

Opera Company of Philadelphia's production of *Salome*, claims that Wilde's poetic style was seen as unoriginal and at times not inspirational. "It was the writer's lecture tour of the United States in 1882 that gave him the confidence to enhance his mediocre writing skills," the article concluded.)

Wilde's lecture tour of America coincided with the production of his first play, *Vera*, in New York City, which was not a success. The 1882 tour took the dapper aesthete to the wilds of Colorado, where he hobnobbed with cowboys and miners. It also took him to 1801 Spruce Street in Philadelphia, where he spent two days and nights. Wilde also visited Walt Whitman in Camden, in a house that was slated for restoration but which was destroyed by arson in 1994.

Biographer A.L. Rowse writes that Wilde "had the fruity generosity of an Irishman, with the un-Irish quality of magnanimity.... He was an actor, always playing to the gallery. He also had a child's sweetness of nature; there was not a grain of malice or ill will in him."

Wilde married in 1884 and had two sons. Critics say he was "straight" until he met the beautiful nobleman, Lord Alfred, the youngest son of the Marquis of Queensberry (the latter, a nasty man from all historical accounts). One of the things Lord Alfred did was introduce Oscar to the pleasures of London's rent boys.

In 1888, he published *The Happy Prince and Other Tales*, a collection of stories he wrote for his sons. *Dorian Gray* followed in 1890. His second play, *The Duchess of Padua*, was criticized as being "uninspired." Wilde found his theatrical voice at the height of his romance with Lord Alfred, producing *Lady Windermere's Fan* (1892), *A Woman of No Importance*, (1893) and *The Importance of Being Earnest* in 1895.

In all of his plays, Wilde delighted in attacking England's philistines, but the philistines had their revenge after the Marquis of Queensberry charged Wilde with "posing as a sodomite." Unfortunately, Wilde sued the Marquis for libel. This focused so much attention on Wilde that he was charged under a clause in the criminal law and sentenced to two years' hard labor. After his conviction, it is said that female prostitutes danced in the streets, yet throughout all of these trials, Wilde's relationship with Lord Alfred continued to flourish.

Wilde lived three years after his release from prison but the scandal ended both his marriage and his literary career.

He died of meningitis in Paris in 1898.

RALPH WALDO EMERSON

B orn in 1803, Ralph Waldo Emerson was a son of William Emerson, a minister of the First Unitarian Church of Boston. At age 14, Emerson entered Harvard and likewise became a Unitarian minister after graduating.

Grief-stricken by the sudden death of his first wife in 1832 and filled with religious confusion, Emerson informed his congregation at Second Church of Boston that he was resigning, a decision he'd made, he told them, because he believed the Communion service was a Passover meal not ordained by Scripture. The stunned congregation was so sorry to see him go they insisted on supporting him financially for about a year. Soon after that, the 29-year-old left for Europe, where he cultivated his nature philosophy, and where he met the poets Coleridge, Wordsworth and Thomas Carlyle.

Emerson incorporated his belief that human thought and action proceed from nature in his first book, *Nature* (1836). At that time, he began to make his living as a lecturer, drawing most of his material from his journals. In an address to the Harvard Divinity School, he maintained that the individual's intuitive spiritual experience was of more importance than any formalized liturgy.

"No truly great man, from Jesus Christ down-wards, ever founded a sect. What a view must a man have of this universe, who thinks 'he can swallow it all,' who is not doubly and terribly happy that he can keep it from swallowing him!" Emerson wrote.

Harvard banished Emerson for 30 years because of his views, but conferred on him a doctor of law degree in 1836. In the meantime, Emerson published *The American Scholar* (1837) and *English Traits* (1856). In *Illusions*, (1860), a volume of poetry, Emerson won the admiration of W.B. Yeats. On the political front, he spoke out a-gainst the Fugitive Slave Act of 1850, saying, "Christians quote the Bible, quote Paul, quote Christ to justify slavery. If slavery is good, then is lying, theft, arson, homicide each and all good, and to be maintained by the Union societies?"

His friend, pro-slavery advocate, Thomas Carlyle, denounced Emerson at this time. Conversely, Emerson denounced Abraham Lincoln as weak, and once said, "You cannot refine Mr. Lincoln's taste, or extend his horizon."

In an 1820 journal entry, while still a senior at Harvard, Emerson wrote of a "strange face in the freshman class whom I should like to know very much. He has a great deal of character in his features...I shall endeavor to become acquainted with him...."

The man, according to Jonathan Katz in *Gay American History*, was Martin Gay. Emerson wrote: "I began to believe in the Indian doctrine of eye fascination.... We have had already two or three long profound stares at each other. Be it wise or weak or superstitious, I must know him."

After they met, Emerson wrote a short poem about Gay:

I love thee more than women love
And pure and warm and equal in the feeling.

The friendship helped Emerson appreciate Shakespeare's sonnets. "Those addressed to a beautiful young man, seem to show some singular friendship amounting almost to a passion which probably excited Shakespeare's youthful imagination," he wrote.

Though his affection for Gay was to pale, Emerson stated, "To this day, our glance at meeting is not that of indifferent persons...."

In 1835, he moved to Concord, Massachusetts, where he married Lydia Jackson, and where he maintained close ties with Hawthorne, Thoreau and feminist Margaret Fuller.

Food for thought at any rate.

W.H. AUDEN
and CHESTER KALLMAN

When Chester Kallman went to poet W.H. Auden's hotel room the morning after Auden read before the Austrian Society of Literature, he knew something was wrong when his knock went unanswered.

The date—Sept. 29, 1974—would haunt him the rest of his life. His lover and artistic collaborator—in the eyes of many critics one of the finest English poets of the 20th century—had died of heart failure.

"For Chester, life without Wystan was unimaginable, unmanageable, and he wept as though everything he had ever known or remembered or believed about love had come flooding over him," writes Thekla Clark, author of *Wystan and Chester*.

Born in York, England, in 1907 to George and Constance Auden, Wystan was the third of three sons. As a child, he was fascinated by science. While a student at Christ Church, Oxford, he developed a passion for English literature. After college, 45 copies of his first collection of poems was published by poet Stephen Spender. In 1938, the future winner of the National Medal for Literature and Pulitzer Prize left England for

Berlin, then the most liberated city in Europe. In Berlin, Auden met novelist Christopher Isherwood before returning home to work as a schoolmaster.

Kallman was just 18 years old when he met Auden at a poetry reading. The year was 1939. Auden had already attracted the attention of T.S. Eliot with *Poems,* his first commercially printed book. He was also a newly naturalized citizen of the United States, something many Britons considered an act of cowardice in light of the coming World War.

Kallman, whose intention was to wink at Auden during the reading, quickly changed his mind when the disheveled-looking poet began reading his elegy to Yeats, heckling "Miss Mess!" instead. An introduction by Isherwood followed, and by their second date, the two men had become lovers.

Kallman, according to poet Harold Norse, had an androgynous appeal: "Willowy grace combined with a deep, manly voice. Not at all effeminate, just young, blond; he was tall, unathletic, with slightly stooped shoulders...."

"Mr. Right has come into my life," wrote Auden to his brother. "He is a Romanian American Jew called Chester Kallman, 18, extremely intelligent and, I think, about to become a good poet."

Their contrasting personalities—Kallman's comic, irresponsible, agnostic streak vs. Auden's Christian-oriented master/servant view of the world—extended to feelings about being gay. Auden was fixated on Freud's categorization of same-sex love as an "immature" phase. As a devout Anglican of an older era, he had religious reservations about his attraction to men. Kallman, on the other hand, saw homosexuality as beautiful and viewed Auden's idea of God's love as off-target. Throughout his life, Auden retained a fascination for all things female, while Kallman was repulsed, as Clark puts it, "by heterosexual goings-on."

Theirs was a potent dynamic. Auden as essayist depended on Kallman's critical judgment. They might argue over Hart Crane's poetry, or get into a screaming match on the street over some literary subject. This tension heightened their 30-year collaboration on a number of opera librettos, including an English libretto for Igor Stravinski's *Rake's Progress*, Nicolas Nabokov's *Love's Labour's Lost*, a translation of Mozart's *The Magic Flute* and the antimasque *The Entertainment of the Senses* for music by John Gardner.

Kallman, in fact, helped Auden become one of the greatest love poets of the 20th century, despite the difficulties of their nonmonogamous union. Auden, who loved to quote Antoine de Saint-Exupery — "Love does not consist of gazing at each other but in looking together in the same direction — regarded his marriage to Kallman as "sacramental." Early in their relationship, he wrote, "The memory of the bliss of Paradise is what gives us the courage to enter Purgatory again with hope to regain it."

While Kallman had other passionate attachments during his time with Auden, these trysts were but blips on a heart graph that held only one name: Wystan Hugh Auden. Kallman was at such a loss after Auden's death that many believe Kallman's demise two years later was caused by a broken heart.

Remembering
ALLEN GINSBERG

In May of 1995 Allen Ginsberg celebrated the release
of *Journals, 1954-1958* (Harper Collins). This was
Ginsberg's third published journal notebook. *Indian
Journals*, an account of the poet's time in India with
Peter Orlovsky in the sixties, was issued in 1970. Grove
Press reprinted a second journal from the early '50s and
'60s. Lost are journals from the mid-'50s. These 1954-
1958 journals were later found and published in 1995.

The 1954-1958 journals cover the period when
Ginsberg lived with Neal Cassidy ("the cocksman and
Adonis of Denver," Ginsberg writes in *Howl*), his odys-
sey to San Jose and then to San Francisco, where the
young poet found work and met poets Gary Snyder,
Kenneth Rexroth and Philip Whelan of the San
Francisco poetry renaissance.

Ginsberg told me that the '54-'58 journals contain a
long description of a love torment involving Neal Cassidy ("NC" in his poems) with one scene taking place in
front of Cassidy's wife. There are details of his first
meeting (and wooing of) the hard-to-catch Peter Orlovsky, their eventual spiritual marriage, his trip to Tangier
and stay with William Burroughs to help put together

Naked Lunch, a year's stay in Paris, then back to the U.S. "It was," Ginsberg said, "an exciting period."

1995 wasn't bad either, judging from the reissuing of three of his books. Fresh off the press were *White Shroud (1980-1985)*, *Cosmopolitan Greetings (1985-1992)*, and the big coffee table-annotated *Howl*.

Before his death in 1997, Ginsberg was Distinguished Professor of English at Brooklyn College, City University of New York. Finally, he was no longer an outlaw among academic poets. He also continued to make big leaps into popular culture, especially with the release of a four CD box set of poems and songs from 1949 onward.

The national gay bard was both reflective and diet conscious when I spoke to him by phone in 1995. He told me he was eating no-salt oatmeal with Chinese mushrooms, fried turnips, seaweed, and plenty of Japanese herbs and vegetables. He'd eaten a mango before our interview and was hard at work with his pen and Chinese ink, writing captions for a photo show.

Health problems were a major concern for him then. He told me he took medication for high blood pressure, and that diabetes made it hard for him to get an erection "unless," he emphasized, "I get a lot of help." He told me that he still liked to make love to young men and that he had several boyfriends. "I'm doing okay in this department. There's a 19-year-old who made it with me and who I have a crush on."

"I'm amazed that he likes me," he said, in a voice that was as melodious as a soft chant.

At the time of our conversation, Ginsberg's partner of many decades, Peter Orlovsky, was in a rehab center in Atlanta for alcohol addiction, but Ginsberg mentioned being in constant communication with Orlovsky's caseworker.

His membership in the American Academy of Arts and Letters was marred by the work of what he called "neo-conservative censorists and right-wing fanatics."

"The same poetry that students read during the day in the Norton Anthology is banned from being broadcast in my voice on the radio from 6 a.m. to 8 p.m., the hours students are studying them," he said.

It wasn't only Ginsberg's voice that was banned from the radio. It's all so-called indecent language, the result of a law drawn up by Senator Jesse Helms that became FCC law in October 1988. Ginsberg helped organize a legal contest with William Burroughs, the ACLU, and the Pen Club, a national writers' organization. "We busted them halfway. There's not a safe harbor between 8 P.M. and 6 A.M. where anything can be read," he said.

When Ginsberg heard that the FCC wanted to eliminate the safe harbor hours, his group petitioned the Supreme Court. After a series of complicated legal maneuvers, the case was shuffled to the lower courts. Fed up, Ginsberg went to Washington to read *Howl* on the steps of the Appeals Court. The FCC did retain the "safe harbor" hours between 10 p.m. and 6 a.m.

"People in America and Europe are not aware that there is *legal*, not *self*-censorship on the air now," he said. "They think it's self-censorship. Helms himself put the law in and it was signed by Reagan. The main marketplace of ideas now is radio and TV since people don't read much anymore. Helms had interfered with the free market. His original contention when he attacked Mapplethorpe was to try and save government money from dirty use. But he has extended it to listener supported, non-government supported stations and this is total censorship."

He accused the right wing of using the same kind of language that Stalin used. Questions like, "Why should the government have to pay for elitist, individualist art?" or "Why should the taxpayer have to put up with this spiritual corruption?" or "Why should degenerate art be funded by the government?" have totalitarian correlations, he said.

"'Spiritual corruption' comes from Mao Tse Tung. 'Elitist individualism' comes from Stalin. 'Degenerate art' comes from Hitler's vocabulary. The right wing has a totalitarian motive because they think they speak for God."

All of which made no sense to the Buddhist Ginsberg. "The concept of a central divinity is a Western idea. As a Buddhist, I've come to realize there's no reason for this kind of centralization and hierarchy, so it's even more ridiculous to hear some Bible thumper claiming to speak for a Central Personality in the Universe."

About the LGBT movement, Ginsberg said that the one development that disturbed him the most was the attack on the North American Man-Boy Love Association (NAMBLA).

"The Helms law which targets gay organizations with ties to NAMBLA is unfair. The most ancient gay tradition is the love of young boys. At the Vatican museum, or any museum really, you see Greek statuary, you see young kids, 14 to 16. That's the ideal model. In Tibetan Buddhism when you visualize a sexual deity it's usually a 15-year-old boy with blue skin representing the emptiness of the blue sky. The appreciation of youth like that is human and universal, just very ordinary."

"NAMBLA is an appreciation and a discussion group; it's not a sex or rape club. For the respectable gay movement to allow itself to be split on this issue instead of taking a more humane and humorous view is a political mistake."

Ginsberg also felt that many (at that time, twentysomething) Generation X'ers were alienated from their own feelings. "They have the attitude, 'I'm a loser, so why don't you kill me?' The one element missing among them is the delight and grief and tears and the emotion. The political key is the restoration of emotion, they need to get in touch with feelings of vulnerability, emotion and grief."

The bard advised straight men to make out with their best friend if there's "an inclination and some kind of heartthrob," but he wouldn't want to categorize this as having a homosexual experience. "Some straight men are close to the experience, they'd be willing but they don't have the impulse. Some have a little softness for men as well as the impulse. Everybody is different from everybody else. It's a little like fingerprints."

On the day of the interview, Ginsberg told me that he was busy calling friends about a poetry reading he was doing with musician Steven Taylor at New York University's Loeb Center. He was excited about the joint performance, he said, because he's had a crush on Taylor for 20 years. "Taylor has a girlfriend but our lovemaking resonates in the music," he said. Then he mentioned an uptown gathering for a Nobel Prize winner, and dinner out with friends and "whoever else might be available."

GINSBERG and ORLOVSKY
Celebrity in Sex, Drugs, Art and Iconoclasm

Poet Allen Ginsberg and Peter Orlovsky broke all the rules when they became a couple.

Ginsberg, despite myriad experiences with women, was gay; Orlovsky was heterosexual. Their attraction led to an exchange of vows in a San Francisco cafeteria. Of that 1955 moment, Ginsberg wrote: "We made a vow to each other that he could own me...so that we possessed each other as property, to do anything we wanted to." Their union, which lasted more than 30 years, allowed Orlovsky to pursue women and Ginsberg to sleep with other men. Jack Kerouac, William Burroughs and Neal Cassidy fell into this category, though occasionally Ginsberg and Orlovsky threw big parties where everybody, male and female, wound up in the same bed.

Ginsberg was born in 1926 to Louis and Naomi Ginsberg. It took Ginsberg 10 years to find a publisher for his first volume of poetry, *Empty Mirror*. Later, in a squalid room in East Harlem, the poet heard the voice of mystic and poet William Blake reciting the poem, "Ah,

Sunflower." The transforming moment would stay with him forever.

Orlovsky was born in 1933 in New York's Lower East Side. Poverty forced him to ditch college for a brief stint in the army. Gifted, as was his mother Katherine, "with large hands," Orlovsky worked menial jobs in psychiatric institutions until long after he and Ginsberg rented an apartment together in New York City. Both men became well-known writers in what came to be called the Beat Movement.

The two men became public icons when Ginsberg's historic San Francisco reading of his masterpiece, "Howl," brought him into the limelight and put the term "The Beat Generation" on the covers of magazines like *Time* and *Life*. Ginsberg was soon traveling everywhere with Orlovsky: The pair visited Paris (where they met Celine and Marcel Duchamp) and Tangier (where Ginsberg kissed Ezra Pound). Then came meetings with Timothy Leary and experiments with psilocybin mushrooms, and the infamous 1968 Democratic Convention where the two lovers, along with Jean Genet, Norman Mailer and thousands of demonstrators, confronted police riot squads.

Never a dull moment: The lovers headed to India, where, despite the country's bounty of opium dens and red-light districts, Ginsberg shocked students at Hindu University with what Indian police called "profanity." India's spirituality, however, helped Ginsberg become less cerebral. The change was manifested in his poetry, especially in "Kaddish," his tribute to his mother, a poem many commentators consider his best work.

A trip to Cuba in 1965 ended poorly when Ginsberg was deported after speaking out against that government's treatment of homosexuals. In Czechoslovakia, the visiting Ginsberg was elected by 100,000

Prague students as King of the May and paraded through the streets on a portable throne. Czech police, fearful of the poet's influence on youth, escorted him to an airplane that took him out of the country.

The Ginsberg/Orlovksy farm in upstate New York was not only a retreat for artist and writer friends, but also served as an oasis for Orlovsky to dry out between bouts with alcohol, Benzedrine and other drugs. By the mid-1980s, Orlovsky's substance abuse had reached disastrous levels. A bipolar condition, left undiagnosed for years, combined with years of overindulgence, led to mental illness and the dissolution of their partnership.

Ginsberg's 1974 National Book Award in Poetry, his election to the American Academy of Arts and Letters and the 1994 sale of his papers to Stanford University for $1 million left no doubts that he had emerged into the mainstream consciousness.

At the time of Ginsberg's death from liver cancer in 1998, Orlovsky had been sober for a year and was able to be at his side, along with intimate friends and a Buddhist priest. When Ginsberg sat up in bed for the last time, according to reports, "His left arm lifted and extended...his mouth opened, and...he seemed to struggle to say something, but only a soft low sound, a weak 'Aah,' came from him."

WILLIAM BURROUGHS

The writer whom Norman Mailer once called "the only American novelist today who may conceivably be possessed by genius," had a morphine habit as a young man. He also associated with hoodlums in Times Square, rolled drunks in the subway, and horded stolen goods in his apartment.

The writer, William Seward Burroughs, was born in 1914 and educated at Harvard before his life of crime and junk. In 1951, his life changed forever when he shot and killed his wife, Joan Vollmer, while attempting to shoot a wine glass from her head in a game he referred to as "playing William Tell."

It was only after his wife's death that Burroughs got serious about his writing. The tragedy compelled him to visit South America in search of the drug, Yage, and to travel to Tangier, where he lived in a series of male brothels, in rooms with shooting galleries and razor-sharp knives. After the publication of his first book, *Junkie*, in 1953, Burroughs made hashish candy in Tangier and worked on his masterpiece, *Naked Lunch*, composing the book in a sloppy fashion, letting the manuscript pile up on the floor in total disarray.

Friends like Allen Ginsberg and Jack Kerouac followed Burroughs to Morocco. The trip coincided with

Burroughs' affair with Ginsberg, a relationship Ginsberg eventually terminated. Burroughs took Ginsberg's rejection to heart, though soon found comfort in the young men of Tangier. "To the Arabs, homosexuality is a genital thing and doesn't spill over into the concept of a family...it is common for Arabs to have homosexual affairs, but they are casual. It is considered quite normal for Arab men to like women and boys," Burroughs told *Gay Sunshine* in 1979.

Naked Lunch became famous after its publication in 1959 because of its description of drug addiction and its daring homosexual themes—not to mention his utterly brilliant, surrealistic prose. Not since James Joyce's *Ulysses*, and Henry Miller's *Tropic of Cancer* had a book generated so much controversy (it was banned in Massachusetts in 1966). Other Burroughs books followed: *The Exterminator* (1960), *The Soft Machine* (1961), and *The Ticket That Exploded* (1962). By the time *Queer* was published in 1984, Ginsberg was lionizing Burroughs as the real hero of gay liberation. Burroughs, Ginsberg noted, looks at homosexuality "through the eyes of a Sufi or Zen master, or an adept Tibetan monk saying, 'Ah.'"

Burroughs described himself as "a homosexual writer with hardly a woman in his books." In *Gay Sunshine*, he's quoted as saying that matriarchal societies are anti-sexual and specifically anti-homosexual. "The more of a damper there's put on sex in general and the harder it is to get outside marriage, the better chance women have," he said. He also believed in the value of male prostitution. "Homosexuality is a worldwide economic fact; in poor countries, it's one of the big industries, one of the main ways a young boy can get somewhere. In Morocco we have a boy who is working at dull [labor] which will bring him seven dollars a week. He can earn five dollars in ten minutes through sex."

Gay liberation will be victorious, Burroughs wrote in *The Gay Liberation Book* (1973), because "the teachings of Saint Paul are unworkable since the pill has separated sexual pleasure from reproduction," and since "over-population has made reproduction something to be curtailed rather than encouraged."

Burroughs spent his final years in Kansas before his death in 1997 at age 83.

Where Have You Gone,
JACK KEROUAC

Jean-Louis Kerouac was born on March 12, 1922. As a boy he loved the radio show, *The Shadow*, and the novels of Thomas Wolfe. He won a football scholarship to Columbia University but did not play the sport [at Columbia] because he had a falling out with the football coach. At school he hung out with Allen Ginsberg, Lucien Carr and William S. Burroughs. He dropped out of school and wrote *The Town and the City*, a conventional first novel that brought him respect but not the fame he would later receive with *On the Road*, which he wrote after traveling cross-country with Ginsberg's crowd. Met with rejection at every turn, it took Kerouac seven long years to find a publisher for the book, but when it was finally accepted, he became an instant celebrity.

Fame destroyed Kerouac, as he spent the rest of his life trying to recreate the role of the wild young bohemian depicted in *On The Road*. Although he wrote a number of other works, like the novel, *Big Sur*, he retreated into a life of isolation and drinking while living with his mother on Long Island. He became a political conservative and intensely religious [Catholic]. He died on October 21, 1969.

When Paul Goodman wrote *Growing Up Absurd* in the 50s, Jack Kerouac's *On The Road* was the bible of the cool, the hip, the non-conformist. But Goodman analyzed Kerouac's book from the psychosexual perspective, asking: If all these characters are so cool, so revolutionary, so Bohemian and so against the grain of the American puritanical machine, why is it that none of them ever had a passing homosexual experience?

The question was relevant then and it is relevant now, especially considering the re-emergence of *On The Road* among some circles of the very young.

Since Kerouac wrote about poet Allen Ginsberg and Ginsberg's bisexual lover, Neal Cassidy (they were Kerouac's characters Carlo Marx and Dean, respectively), the novel's homoerotic omission seems peculiar. Kerouac himself conducted an on/off-again affair with Ginsberg that is not even hinted at in *On The Road* but is discussed at great length in the Kerouac biographies and in Ginsberg's own talks and writings.

Goodman criticizes the rebellion of these Kerouacian beats by arguing that their experiences were all superficial: drinking, wild parties, stealing cars, and getting laid in the [orthodox] college fraternity manner. Avant-garde and revolutionary? Not on your life!

I was reminded of Goodman's comments while waiting for the subway a couple of years ago, when I saw a college kid oh-so-earnestly reading a copy of *On The Road*. Extremely evocative to me was the fact that a great majority of the young people who read this book today do so without knowing what Kerouac, Ginsberg, Cassidy and Burroughs did when they were not racing from highway to highway.

I couldn't resist; I had to speak with him…find out what makes a 21st Century *On The Road* reader in 2002 tick. I cast a friendly glance at him and mentioned the book. He looked at me in a mildly receptive manner and closed the book, using his fingers as a bookmark.

"Have you ever heard of Allen Ginsberg and William Burroughs?" I asked.

He looked at me as if I had mentioned Pope Benedict XII. "No," he demurred.

"Well, they're all writers who were friends of Kerouac. He writes about them in *On The Road*, but doesn't tell you the whole truth. If you read Ginsberg's poetry—"Kaddish," "Howl," "The Fall of America"—and investigate William Burroughs' *Naked Lunch*, you might get a pretty good picture of what the other half of Kerouac was all about."

The kid nodded his head in a semi-interested fashion, then seemed to withdraw, no doubt sensing that I was trying to tell him something that would make him uncomfortable. And in not-so-gently attempting to gauge the homo and bisexuality recognition factor among the youth of today, I was.

Perhaps he spotted the gay magazine I was carrying, with its cover photograph of two men kissing. In any event, when he noticed the magazine for real, he clammed up immediately and dove back into his Kerouac as if it were the Holy Writ. Jack Kerouac: the guru of do-your-own-thing, of experimentation on all levels, whom Ginsberg praises in explicit sexual terms.

I found that young man's reaction ironic. I mean, hasn't the true meaning of hip always implied a willingness to experiment, to take on the mantle of adventure, to question authority? Even supposing that the lad was on the extreme heterosexual end of the Kinsey scale, his response spoke volumes about the consciousness of today's [heterosexual] young: that they have pulled in the reins at certain types of life experiences, that they have shut the doors on all the adjacent rooms in the labyrinth of true rebellion.

Speaking with a professor of sociology at a local university not long ago only served to corroborate my suspicions.

"You merely mention the word 'homosexual' in a sociological context," he said, "and you can see them [his students] tighten up, wishing you'd stop talking, wishing you'd change the subject. Everything about the look on their faces and their body language cries out to you, begs you to change the subject. They just want to totally ignore it."

I cannot help but feel that this attitude toward homosexuality (ignoring it) is not just the result of society having had to face the reality of AIDS for almost three decades, but the Reagan administration's refusal to even acknowledge it. And the subtle attitudinal setback that really began to take hold in the early 80s has been nothing but reinforced by the regimes of the two "Bush Benitos."

Young people have long since put down their copies of *The Greening of America*, their volumes by Sylvia Plath, the philosophy of Herbert Marcuse, and Herman Hesse novels—all of which have been exchanged for The *Wall Street Journal*, an infosource that most of us in the 60s and 70s wouldn't have been seen carrying under penalty of death—except, perhaps, in a brown paper wrapper.

Anxious to find out if a spirit of revolution might still be alive when I spotted the young man reading Jack Kerouac's *On The Road*, I was loath to confirm my suspicion that he didn't have a clue. Perhaps I should have known better, kept my mouth shut, but what is the likelihood of my running into a young person reading a copy of, let's say, Herman Hesse's *Beneath the Wheel*?

No, jaded idealists have to confirm their disillusionment when the opportunity arises.

ABOUT THE AUTHOR:

Philadelphia-based author/journalist/poet and film critic, Thom Nickels is the author of The *Cliffs of Aries* (1988), *Two Novellas: Walking Water & After All This* (1989, nominated for a 1989 Lambda Literary Award and a 1990 Hugo Award), *The Boy on the Bicycle* (1993-94), *Manayunk* (2001), *Gay and Lesbian Philadelphia* (2002-03), and *Tropic of Libra* (2003). Nickels has written political/social commentary pieces, celebrity interviews, features, book and theater reviews for local and national publications, including *The Philadelphia Inquirer*, The *Philadelphia Daily News*, The *Evening Bulletin, The Gay and Lesbian Worldwide Review* and the *Lambda Book Report*. He is a Contributing Editor for *Philadelphia's Weekly Press*, a weekly columnist for *STAR Publications*, and writes frequently on architecture for *Philadelphia Metro* and The *Evening Bulletin*. His poetry has been featured in *Van Gogh's Ear 2004/2005* (French Connection Press, Paris). Nickels will script *Revelations: The History of Gay and Lesbian Philadelphia*, a documentary film produced by Longshore Films, Inc., about his book of the same title. His photo-history book, *Philadelphia Architecture*, is slated for publication by Arcadia Publishing in late 2005.

BIBLIOGRAPHY

Most of the biographies in this book were published as columns in the *Philadelphia Gay News* in the early to mid-1990s. The longer essays, such as "Carlton Willers" and "Susan Sontag" were originally published in Philadelphia's *Weekly Press*. The essay on Andre Gide, with modifications, originally appeared in *The Gay and Lesbian Review*. "Valerie Solanas" appeared in the *Lambda Book Review*.

Source materials for the biographies and essays include: *Gay American History* (Thomas Y. Crowell Co., 1976); *The Gay and Lesbian Almanac,* Jonathan Katz (Harper & Row, New York, 1983); *Homosexuality in History,* Colin Spencer (Harcourt Brace & Co., New York, 1995); *Sexual Politics,* Kate Millet (Doubleday & Co., New York, 1969); *Lesbian Nation,* Jill Johnston (Simon & Schuster, 1973); *Chapters From an Autobiography,* Samuel M. Steward Grey Fox Press, San Francisco, 1980); *The Poet in America,* Helen Vendler (Random House, New York, 1987); *Professional Secrets,* Jean Cocteau (Farrar, Straus & Giroux, 1970); *Life and Death of Andy Warhol,* Victor Bockris (Bantam Books, 1989); *Winckelmann: Writings on Art* (Phaidon, New York, 1972); *Some Remarkable Men,* James Lord (Farrar, Straus & Giroux, 1996); *Prisoner of Love,* Jean Genet (Wesleyan University Press, 1992); *Walt Whitman on Long Island,* Bertha H. Funnell (Kennikat Press, New York/London, 1971); *Do What Thou Wilt,* Lawrence Sutin (St. Martin's, 2000); *Lincoln and Whitman,* Daniel Mark Epstein (Ballantine Books, New York, 2004); *Susan Sontag,* Carl Rollyson and Lisa Paddock (W. W. & Norton Co., 2000); *Conversations with Susan Sontag;* (various authors, University Press of Mississippi, 1995); *Knowing When to Stop,* Ned Rorem Simon & Schuster, 1994); *The Trouble with Harry Hay,* Stuart

Timmons (Alyson, Boston, 1990); *Stargazer*, Stephen Koch (Calder & Boyars, London, 1973); *Greek Homosexuality*, K. J. Dover (Vintage Books/Knopf, New York, 1980); *The Andre Gide Reader*, David Littlejohn (Knopf, New York, 1971); *Calamus Lovers*, Charley Shively (Gay Sunshine Press, 1987); *The Celluloid Closet*, Vito Russo (Harper & Row, 1981); *Gay Sunshine Interviews*, Winston Leyland (Gay Sunshine Press, 1978); *Homosexuals in History*, A.L. Rowse (Dorset Press, 1977); *Christianity, Social Tolerance, and Homosexuality*, John Boswell (University of Chicago, 1980); *Lesbian Lists*, Dell Richards (Alyson, 1990); *Gore Vidal*, Fred Kaplan (Doubleday, New York, 1999); *Mars Without Venus*, Major-General Frank Richardson (Wm. Blackwood Edinburgh, 1981); *Gay Priest*, Malcolm Boyd (St. Martin's, New York, 1986); *Rimbaud*, Graham Robb (W. W. Norton, 2000); *The Life of D.H. Lawrence*, Keith Sagar (Pantheon Books, New York, 1980); *The Church and the Homosexual*, John J. McNeill, S. J. (Beacon Press, 1993); *Wystan and Chester*, Thekla Clark (Columbia University Press, New York, 1995); *The Naked Civil Servant*, Quentin Crisp (Holt, Rinehart & Winston, New York, 1978); *James Baldwin*, Randall Kenan (Chelsea House, New York, 1994); *Five Years*, Paul Goodman (Vintage Books, New York, 1969); *The Gay Militants*, Donn Teal (Stein and Day, 1971); *Mapplethorpe*, Patricia Morrisroe (Random House, 1995); *Byron*, Benita Eisler (Knopf 1999); *Oscar Wilde*, Richard Ellmann (Vintage Books, 1988); *Keith Haring Journals* (Viking Press, 1996); *The Spirit and the Flesh*, Walter Williams (Beacon, 1986); *Jean Genet in Tangier*, Mohamed Choukri (Ecco Press, New York, 1973); *D. H. Lawrence and Edward Carpenter, A Study in Edwardian Transition*, Emile Delavenay (Taplinger Publishing Co., New York, 1971); *Genet*, Edmund White (Knopf, 1993).